BEST PRACTICE FOR THE TOEIC® L&R TEST

–Advanced–

TOEIC® L&R TEST への総合アプローチ
—Advanced—

YOSHIZUKA Hiroshi

Graham Skerritt

JN062934

写真提供: ©iStockPhoto
ゲッティイメージズ
Shutterstock

音声ファイルのダウンロード／ストリーミング

CD マーク表示がある箇所は、音声を弊社 HP より無料でダウンロード／ストリーミングすることができます。下記 URL の書籍詳細ページに音声ダウンロードアイコンがございますのでそちらから自習用音声としてご活用ください。

https://seibido.co.jp/ad668

BEST PRACTICE FOR THE TOEIC® L&R TEST
—Advanced—

はしがき

　皆さんは「グローバル人材に求められる英語力」とはどんなものか、考えたことはあります
か。様々な回答があって当然だと思いますが、あえて私見を述べるなら、1. 人種や国籍に
こだわらず、相手の発言に耳を傾けることができること。2. 自分と異なる意見を排除するので
はなく、違いとして理解し認められること。3. 自分の考えを明確に相手に伝えられること。
この3つだと考えています。「あれ、英語はどうしたの?」と思った人もいるかもしれません
が、上の3つを実践するための媒介が「英語」です。

　世界の4人にひとりが英語を話すグローバルな時代に私たちはいます。英語はできて当た
り前になりました。さらには、あなたが仕事で英語を使う相手はネイティブよりノンネイティブ
(非英語母語話者) である可能性のほうがはるかに高いのです。ということは様々な発音上
の癖やなまりを聞き取れるようにならなければなりません。世界は正にWorld Englishesの
時代です。10カ国の人がいたらそのうち最低でも7カ国の人の発言は聞き取れるようになりま
しょう。10カ国の人がいたらそのうち最低でも7カ国の人に分かってもらえるような発音がで
きるようになりましょう。

　TOEICで出題される語彙や表現、場面にはグローバルに通用するものが取り上げられて
います。換言すると、英・米・豪・加など英語を母語とする国の文化に依拠するような問題は
極力排除されているということです。皆さんはTOEICというテストを受ける、という目標の先
にあるグローバル人材が身につけるべき英語を知り、学ぶということを視野に入れ、励んで
いただきたいと思います。

　本書の発刊に当たり、『BEST PRACTICE FOR THE TOEIC® L&R TEST』を
BasicからAdvancedまでのシリーズ三部作とすることをご提案いただいた㈱成美堂の佐野
英一郎氏、引き続き編集の労をお取りくださった宍戸貢氏、太田裕美氏、丁寧な英文校閲を
してくださったBill Benfieldの各氏に改めて御礼申し上げます。

2022年秋

吉塚　弘

Graham Skerritt

本書の構成と使い方

■全般：

・全UnitがDining OutやOfficesなどのトピック別の構成になっています。

・各Unitには、Part 1〜Part 7までの全てが収められています。

・各Partの問題は、Unit 1からUnit 14へと出題頻度と重要度の観点から配置されています。

▶Warm up — Dictation Practice：

・リスニングセクションに入る前の耳慣らしです。

・音声は成美堂ホームページ（https://www.seibido.co.jp/ad668）よりダウンロードあるいはスマートフォンやタブレットでストリーミング再生してください。

・日本人にとって聞き取りにくい音の変化を学べるようになっています。聞き取りの際の注意点は、"Points to Dictate"にあります。

・Points to Dictateにあるカタカナは発話の際のガイダンスとしてもご利用いただけます。

☞音声を聞き、空所部分を書き取ってください。音声は何度聞いても構いません。

▶頻出単語チェック！：

・各Unitのトピックに頻出し、当該Unitでも使用されている語句をチェックします。

・リスニングとリーディングの両セクションの最初のページに10語ずつあります。

☞見出し語句と適切な意味（英語）を選びます。意味は本文で使われている意味が表示されています。

▶各Partの構成：

全Partに"Check Point!"があります。何を学ぶのか、どのような能力を身に付ければよいのかを明示しました。

LISTENING SECTION

- Part 1は、He, She, The man, The womanなどに加え人物以外の主語も取り上げています。
- Part 2は、質問文に頻出する疑問詞を中心とした構成になっています。
- Part 3は、会話の内容や目的、誰

と誰の会話かなどの概略を問う質問文を例題の最初に取り上げています。2名の会話だけではなく3名の会話を聞いて解答する問題や、図表を見ながら解答する問題、話し手の意図を問う問題もUnit 7以降に採用しています。

- Part 4は、説明文の主旨や主題、目的などの概略を問う質問文を問題の最初に取り上げています。音声と印刷された図表の情報を関連づけて解答する質問と、話し手の意図を問う質問もUnit 9以降に採用しています。

☞ Warm up同様に音声は成美堂ホームページ (https://www.seibido.co.jp/ad668) よりダウンロードあるいはスマートフォンやタブレットでストリーミング再生してください。

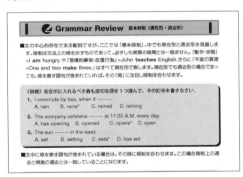

▶Grammar Review：

- 文法項目を頻度順に復習します。

☞各項目の説明を読み、続く例題に取り組みましょう。

READING SECTION

- Part 5は、5つの問題のうち、最初の3つが文法問題、残り2つが語彙問題です。文法問題は前ページのGrammar Reviewで学んだ内容が問われています。語彙問題は頻度の高い品詞を取り上げています。
- Part 6は、4つの空所のうち、3つは文法問題と語彙問題で、1つが文挿入問題です。

・Part 7は、出題頻度の高いEメールやメモ、手紙、広告文などを取り上げています。それぞれの説明文の主旨や主題、目的などの概略を問う質問文が問題の最初に出題されています。また、最近出題されるようになったテキストメッセージやオンラインチャット形式の問題や3つの文書を読んで解答する問題、さらに書き手の意図を問う質問や1文を挿入する文挿入問題を採用しています。

☞ Part 5〜Part 7までは、目安の制限時間を設けて取り組みましょう。

　Part 5 ---- 3分45秒（45秒@1問）

　Part 6 ---- 3分20秒（50秒@1問）

　Part 7 ---- 1分40秒（50秒@1問）←1つの文書

　　　　　　 5分00秒（60秒@1問）←2つの文書

　　　　　　 6分40秒（80秒@1問）←3つの文書

◎TOEIC重要熟語100

　巻末付録として「TOEIC重要熟語100」を付けました。知っている単語が2つ以上並ぶと知らない単語に変身してしまいます。リスニングの一瞬で聞こえたり、リーディングの一部に登場すると「何のこと?」となってそれ以降の音声が聞けなくなったり、読めなくなったりします。✔ボックスを付けておきましたので、知らないものがあったら必ず覚えましょう。

●TESTUDY

本書ではTESTUDY（=TEST+STUDY）という「e-learning+オンラインテスト」システムがご利用いただけます。

1. e-Learning：各Unitの復習ができます。（標準学習時間=30分）

2. Unit Review：各Unitのリスニングセクションをベースにしたディクテーション問題です。（標準学習時間=15分）

3. 「TOEIC重要熟語100」も選択形式で学べます。

4. Extra Test：オンラインテストです。（標準学習時間=50分）

☞全て教員の指示に従って学習・受験してください。

目 次

Dining Out

:: Warm up　　　Dictation Practice　🔊 1-02

それぞれの空所に入る語句を、音声を聞いて書き入れてみましょう。ただし、短縮形が含まれる場合は短縮形で記入しましょう。

1. I've booked a really _____ at the restaurant.
2. Would you like _____ wine, Mr. Martin?
3. All of the desserts _____ to me, but I'll have the fruit salad.
4. We usually _____ to a traditional French restaurant.
5. If you're having a starter, I recommend the chicken and _____.
6. I'm sorry but we _____ credit cards.
7. _____, I'll take you to a great Italian restaurant.
8. John's retirement party _____ a lot of fun.
9. You _____ pay for your own food.
10. Do you want to get a sandwich or would you prefer some _____?

🔍 Points to Dictate

1 語目の語尾と 2 語目の語頭が似た音や発音しにくい 2 語が連続しているとき、発音しにくいので間の 1 音が脱落して発音されます。脱落する代わりにそこに 1 字分のポーズが置かれます（以後ポーズを [ ] と表記）。
さまざまな音の脱落を体験し、同類の変化に対する対応力をつけましょう。

✅ 頻出単語チェック！　Listening Section

語句と意味を品詞に気をつけながら結びつけてみましょう。

1. banquet
2. confirmation
3. attendee
4. reminder
5. extremely
6. cancel [v.]
7. at short notice
8. refund [v.]
9. deposit [n.]
10. get in touch

a. some money paid in advance as part of the total amount
b. to return the money that someone paid for something
c. agreement that something is true or certain
d. to contact
e. a very short time before
f. very
g. a message to tell people to remember to do something
h. a person attending an event
i. to decide not to do something
j. a large formal meal

PART 1　写真描写問題

 1-03, 04

> ***Check Point!*** ＼ 2人のそれぞれの動作に注目しましょう。
> **She** と **He** は人物が特定される場合に使われます。

それぞれの写真について、4つの説明文の中から最も適切なものを1つずつ選びましょう。

1.

Ⓐ Ⓑ Ⓒ Ⓓ

2.

Ⓐ Ⓑ Ⓒ Ⓓ

PART 2　応答問題

 1-05-09

> ***Check Point!*** ＼ 質問文の最初の語句、疑問詞などに最大の注意を払いましょう。
> <u>**How long**</u> have you been ～ ing?

それぞれの設問の応答として最も適切なものを1つずつ選びましょう。

3. Mark your answer on your answer sheet.　　　　Ⓐ Ⓑ Ⓒ

4. Mark your answer on your answer sheet.　　　　Ⓐ Ⓑ Ⓒ

5. Mark your answer on your answer sheet.　　　　Ⓐ Ⓑ Ⓒ

6. Mark your answer on your answer sheet.　　　　Ⓐ Ⓑ Ⓒ

7. Mark your answer on your answer sheet.　　　　Ⓐ Ⓑ Ⓒ

PART 3   会話問題   1-10, 11

Check Point! ＼ 全体を問う質問文は定型が多いので頭に入れておきましょう。
What are the speakers discussing?

会話についての設問に対し、最も適切なものを 1 つずつ選びましょう。

8. What are the speakers discussing?
   (A) A social event
   (B) A business trip
   (C) A meeting
   (D) A business deal

9. Where will the speakers go on Friday?
   (A) To another company
   (B) To a bar
   (C) To New York
   (D) To a restaurant

10. What does the woman ask the man to do?
    (A) Meet her at the bar
    (B) Order drinks at the bar
    (C) Pay for his meal
    (D) Remind her about the meal

PART 4   説明文問題   1-12, 13

Check Point! ＼ 誰が誰に発しているメッセージなのかをまず聞き取りましょう。
Who is the message intended for?

説明文についての設問に対し、最も適切なものを 1 つずつ選びましょう。

11. Who is the message intended for?
    (A) A customer who made a reservation
    (B) A guest at a dinner party
    (C) A person who is ill
    (D) A receptionist at a restaurant

12. What problem does the speaker have?
    (A) Her group needs a bigger table.
    (B) Her party has to change time.
    (C) Her friend is feeling sick.
    (D) Her reservation was canceled.

13. What does the speaker ask the listener to do?
    (A) Cancel the reservation
    (B) Reserve a table for another day
    (C) Refund the deposit
    (D) Call her back

■名詞（句）の**前**に**置**かれその名詞（句）を修飾するので**前置詞**です。

必ず「前置詞＋名詞（句）」というセットの形で使われ動詞、名詞、形容詞、副詞、文全体などを修飾します。主語や動詞、目的語にはなりません。

Michael is going to visit the restaurant *with* his friend *on* Friday.

（Michael は金曜日に友人とそのレストランに行く予定です）

２つの前置詞＋名詞（句）はどちらも動詞 visit を修飾しています。

Many guests attended the party in the restaurant ------- the rain.

(A) despite　　(B) without　　(C) unless　　(D) while

空所の後は冠詞＋名詞の名詞句です。従って空所には前置詞しか入らないので接続詞である unless と while は選択肢から外れます。接続詞の後には節が続きます。

例文では（雨にもかかわらずたくさんの客がレストランでのパーティーに参加した）という意味を表す、despite が正解です。

選択肢に前置詞のみならず、接続詞が混ざったものがありますのでしっかり見極めます。

《例題》次の空所に入れるべき最も適切な語を選んで、その記号を書きなさい。

Cathy and Lisa decided to try the new French restaurant ------- 357 Enward Road.

(A) when　　(B) at　　(C) on　　(D) that

☑ 頻出単語チェック！　Reading Section

語句と意味を品詞に気をつけながら結びつけてみましょう。

1. authentic
2. reasonably
3. weekday
4. buffet [n.]
5. magnificent
6. appetizer
7. outdated
8. show signs of
9. relocate
10. cater to

a. old and unfashionable
b. to provide something for some particular people
c. in a good way
d. the first part of a meal; a starter
e. to move from one place to another
f. a meal where people serve themselves from lots of choices
g. seems partly
h. very good
i. real
j. a day between Monday and Friday

Reading Section

PART 5　短文穴埋め問題

Check Point!　文法問題：前置詞、語彙問題：名詞
4つの選択肢を見て判断するが、前置詞以外の品詞があるものに注意。

それぞれの空所に入れるのに最も適切なものを1つずつ選びましょう。

14. The number of fast food restaurants in this city has increased dramatically ------- the past 10 years.
(A) among
(B) behind
(C) over
(D) than
Ⓐ Ⓑ Ⓒ Ⓓ

15. ------- changing the menu, the restaurant was still not attracting enough customers.
(A) Despite
(B) When
(C) As much as
(D) Besides
Ⓐ Ⓑ Ⓒ Ⓓ

16. Marie noticed that the server was walking ------- them with their food.
(A) at
(B) for
(C) in
(D) toward
Ⓐ Ⓑ Ⓒ Ⓓ

17. My local restaurant has started selling some vegetarian -------.
(A) ideas
(B) options
(C) answers
(D) menus
Ⓐ Ⓑ Ⓒ Ⓓ

18. This is a great recipe because it includes lots of nutritious -------.
(A) elements
(B) components
(C) ingredients
(D) constituents
Ⓐ Ⓑ Ⓒ Ⓓ

> **Check Point!**
>
> 語彙問題：動詞
> 文章挿入問題：前段落と比較すると入るべき情報が見えてきます。

それぞれの空所に入れるのに最も適切なものを1つずつ選びましょう。

To:	Maddison Turner<mturner@freemail.com>
From:	Elena Suarez<elenas@acom.com>
Date:	September 20
Subject:	Re: Restaurant recommendations

Dear Maddison,

I'd be happy to suggest some restaurants for your trip to LA.

If you like Mexican food, go to Casa Mexico in East Hollywood. It's run by a Mexican family, so the food is really authentic. It's pretty reasonably ------- **19.**, too.

Another good place, especially on a weekday, is Beijing Diner. The lunch buffet is great value and really good, too. ------- **20.**.

If you want to ------- **21.** people, try the Elysian Grill. The food is magnificent – particularly the steaks. If you decide to get an appetizer, ------- **22.** highly recommend the salmon mousse.

Have a great trip!

Elena

19. (A) price
(B) priced
(C) prices
(D) pricey

20. (A) That's also in East Hollywood.
(B) It's expensive, but it's worth it.
(C) So I don't actually go there very often.
(D) They're only open in the evenings though.

21. (A) inspire
(B) inspect
(C) impact
(D) impress

22. (A) I will
(B) I am
(C) I would
(D) I have

PART 7 読解問題

> **Check Point!** レビュー（1つの文書、2つの質問）
> 1行目でおおよそ何の論評でどのような展開になるか予測できます。

文章を読んで、それぞれの設問の答えとして最も適切なものを1つずつ選びましょう。

Review: Henry's

My first impression of the Henry's was not a good one. The building looked old, the wallpaper was outdated and the furniture in need of replacing. It was also hard to find and a long way from the city center. With low expectations, we asked for a table for two, which was no problem – the restaurant was completely empty.

When the food came, I was pleasantly surprised. The steak was well cooked, and the vegetables were fresh and delicious. My partner was also impressed. Her fish was beautifully fried and presented. In fact, the food was fantastic.

So, despite the location and the interior, Henry's actually shows signs of being a very good restaurant. The owner, local businessman Henry Ford, badly needs to redo the interior and buy some new furniture. However, I strongly suggest relocating to a more modern building in the center of the city. I can easily imagine Henry's catering to crowds of business professionals at lunchtime, and in the evenings, too. Sadly, in its current location and with its current look, few people are likely to walk through the door, which is a shame – because the food is actually outstanding.

23. What is indicated about Henry's?
    (A) It has a good interior and good food.
    (B) It has a good interior but the food is not good.
    (C) It doesn't have a good interior or good food.
    (D) It doesn't have a good interior, but the food is good.

24. What is suggested about the restaurant building?
    (A) It's in a good location for business professionals.
    (B) It is far from the center of the city.
    (C) It needs a better sign.
    (D) It is very modern.

Offices

Warm up　　Dictation Practice 1-14

それぞれの空所に入る語句を、音声を聞いて書き入れてみましょう。

1. She's not at her desk, so she _____ on her lunch break.
2. It's my job to _____ learn the new system.
3. Are you free at 11 A.M. for a _____?
4. Can we talk _____ the new staff?
5. It _____ great to see you at the conference.
6. I have some _____ about the project.
7. Can you help me _____ printer? It's not working.
8. Could you _____ of these documents?
9. The bathroom is _____ there, on the left.
10. I've tried calling them _____, but there's no answer.

 Points to Dictate

1のマストビーはナチュラルスピードで発音されるとマストのトが脱落しマス[ ]ビーのように発音されます。以下、ヘル[ ]ピーポー、クイッ[ ]チャット、アバウ[ ]トレイニング、ウッ[ ]ビー、グッ[ ]ニューズ、ウィ[ ]ザ、メイ[ ]コピーズ、ジャス[ ]ダウン、エイ[ ]タイムズとなります。

✓ 頻出単語チェック!　Listening Section

語句と意味を品詞に気をつけながら結びつけてみましょう。

1. update [n.]
2. scan [v.]
3. check with
4. temporarily
5. behind schedule
6. ahead of time
7. workload
8. management
9. expand
10. assistance

a. early
b. to ask
c. help
d. the amount of work someone must do
e. the latest information
f. the people that are in charge at a company
g. to use a machine to make a digital copy of a document
h. to make something bigger
i. late; not following the plan
j. for a short time

Listening Section

PART 1　写真描写問題　 1-15, 16

> ***Check Point!***　2人のそれぞれの動作に注目しましょう。
> 主語が She と He ではなく The woman と The man です。

それぞれの写真について、4つの説明文の中から最も適切なものを1つずつ選びましょう。

1.

Ⓐ Ⓑ Ⓒ Ⓓ

2.

Ⓐ Ⓑ Ⓒ Ⓓ

PART 2　応答問題　 1-17-21

> ***Check Point!***　質問文の時制と異なる時制の選択肢に注意しましょう。
> <u>Did Manuel</u> ship the orders 〜 ? → <u>He's processing</u> 〜 .

それぞれの設問の応答として最も適切なものを1つずつ選びましょう。

3. Mark your answer on your answer sheet.　Ⓐ Ⓑ Ⓒ

4. Mark your answer on your answer sheet.　Ⓐ Ⓑ Ⓒ

5. Mark your answer on your answer sheet.　Ⓐ Ⓑ Ⓒ

6. Mark your answer on your answer sheet.　Ⓐ Ⓑ Ⓒ

7. Mark your answer on your answer sheet.　Ⓐ Ⓑ Ⓒ

> *Check Point!*　細部を問う質問のみの問題に注意しましょう。
> **What does the woman want the man to do?**

会話についての設問に対し、最も適切なものを1つずつ選びましょう。

8. What does the woman want the man to do?
(A) Tell her about his progress
(B) Sign a contract
(C) Update some software
(D) Give her the scanner

9. What problem does the man mention?
(A) The scanner is broken.
(B) The IT department won't help them.
(C) They need more equipment.
(D) One of the people on the team is slow.

10. What will the woman most likely do next?
(A) Ask Susan to help the man
(B) Call someone in the IT department
(C) Make a new schedule
(D) Borrow someone from another department

> *Check Point!*　話し手と聞き手の関係性を把握しましょう。
> **Who most likely are the listeners?**

説明文についての設問に対し、最も適切なものを1つずつ選びましょう。

11. Who most likely are the listeners?
(A) The heads of departments
(B) New members of staff
(C) Customer service assistants
(D) All the staff at a company

12. What issues does the speaker mention?
(A) People had a lot of work.
(B) Sales results have not been good.
(C) Some people quit the company.
(D) The office is not big enough.

13. What is the company planning to do?
(A) Ask the heads of departments to help staff
(B) Give everyone some time off in June
(C) Expand the office
(D) Hire four new members of staff

✎ Grammar Review 形容詞

■名詞を修飾するのは**形容詞**ですが、3つの形があることを整理しておきましょう。

①**形容詞**：代表的な語尾の形を覚えておきましょう。-able (valu*able*), -al (financi*al*), -ful (meaning*ful*), -ic (optimist*ic*), -ical (crit*ical*), -ive (posit*ive*), -less (use*less*) などがあります。

②**形容詞化した現在分詞**：動詞の -ing 形で「〜するような、〜している」のように能動や進行を表し、後に続く名詞を修飾します。= an amaz*ing* discovery（驚くような発見）、a bark*ing* dog（吠えている犬）。

③**形容詞化した過去分詞**：動詞の過去分詞 (-ed) が形容詞として名詞を修飾し、「〜された、〜してしまった」という受け身・完了を表します。= sophisticat*ed* technology（洗練された技術）、a retir*ed* person（退職した人）。

《例題》各空所に入れるべき最も適切な語を選んで、その記号を書きなさい。

1. Emma bought a ------- chair for her home office.

   (A) comfort　　(B) comfortable　　(C) comfortably　　(D) comforted

2. What is the most ------- part about starting your own company?

   (A) appeal　　(B) appealed　　(C) appealing　　(D) appealingly

3. Tim was offered a job by a newly ------- trading company.

   (A) establish　　(B) establishes　　(C) establishing　　(D) established

---

✔ 頻出単語チェック！　Reading Section

語句と意味を品詞に気をつけながら結びつけてみましょう。

1. notify	a. leaving a place because it is dangerous
2. procedure	b. information about how to use something
3. instructions	c. to throw away
4. supervise	d. the official steps to follow
5. evacuation	e. to introduce (a new rule)
6. in order to	f. so that
7. dispose	g. to watch and check someone's work
8. implement [v.]	h. to avoid doing something
9. refrain from	i. very important
10. crucial	j. to tell someone

PART 5 短文穴埋め問題

Check Point! 文法問題：形容詞、語彙問題：名詞
語根が同一のものであれば語尾から品詞を特定しましょう。

それぞれの空所に入れるのに最も適切なものを1つずつ選びましょう。

14. Everyone was really impressed with the newly ------- office.
(A) decorate
(B) decorated
(C) decorating
(D) decoration
Ⓐ Ⓑ Ⓒ Ⓓ

15. It had been a very ------- trip – all the customers they visited had signed contracts.
(A) fruit
(B) fruitful
(C) fruitless
(D) fruity
Ⓐ Ⓑ Ⓒ Ⓓ

16. The CEO gave a very ------- speech about how good ideas can come from anyone.
(A) motivate
(B) motivated
(C) motivating
(D) motivation
Ⓐ Ⓑ Ⓒ Ⓓ

17. John sent a ------- to the people who had not submitted their paperwork yet.
(A) memory
(B) member
(C) reply
(D) reminder
Ⓐ Ⓑ Ⓒ Ⓓ

18. You need to get ------- from your manager if you want to work overtime.
(A) permission
(B) preparation
(C) application
(D) indication
Ⓐ Ⓑ Ⓒ Ⓓ

PART 6 | 長文穴埋め問題

Check Point! | 語彙問題：前置詞／動詞
文章挿入問題：直前に " One is 〜 " とあるので、これに続くものは？

それぞれの空所に入れるのに最も適切なものを 1 つずつ選びましょう。

To: All Staff Members <allstaff@bates.com>
From: Miriam Knowles <miriam@bates.com>
Date: March 3
Subject: Fire Drill

Dear All,

I am writing to notify you that there will be a fire drill this week. I also want to remind you of the correct procedure ------- follow.
19.

When the alarm sounds, calmly walk to a fire exit. One is located next to the elevator. -------. Do not take the elevator. Walk down the stairs and ------- at the
20. **21.**
meeting point in the car park. Wait there for further ------- from our fire safety
22.
leader, Jonas Braun, who will be supervising the evacuation.

If anyone has any questions, please do not hesitate to ask.

Best regards,

Miriam Knowles
Health and Safety Officer

---

19. (A) for
(B) on
(C) to
(D) with

20. (A) Two are next to the kitchen.
(B) However, remember not to use the elevator.
(C) Second, use the ones near the kitchen.
(D) The other is to the right of the kitchen.

21. (A) assemble
(B) construct
(C) collaborate
(D) organize

22. (A) instructions
(B) instruments
(C) inspections
(D) inclusions

文章を読んで、それぞれの設問の答えとして最も適切なものを1つずつ選びましょう。

Notice: Recycling Bins

In order to reduce waste and contribute to our efforts to become a greener company, we have installed new recycling bins around the office. Before you dispose of any trash, please check carefully that you are using the correct bin.

Each bin has a distinctive color to help you remember to use the right one:

- blue = paper
- green = food waste
- yellow = bottles and cans
- red = plastic

The blue and red bins can be found next to the photocopier and in reception, whereas the green bin is in the kitchen and the yellow one is next to the elevator.

However, please remember that we recently implemented a new policy about the use of paper. This policy requests that you refrain from printing out any documents unless absolutely necessary, and if you must print something out, make sure to print on both sides.

It's crucial that we all work together to make sure we are doing our part for the environment.

Thank you for your cooperation.

23. What is the purpose of this notice?

    (A) To inform staff about some new equipment

    (B) To order staff to recolor the recycling bins

    (C) To thank staff for recycling their waste

    (D) To warn staff about following the rules

24. What does the notice indicate about the company?

    (A) They want to save money by reducing waste.

    (B) They want to be seen as environmentally friendly.

    (C) They made the changes due to staff requests.

    (D) They have always been a green company.

General Business

それぞれの空所に入る語句を、音声を聞いて書き入れてみましょう。ただし、短縮形が含まれる場合は短縮形で記入しましょう。

1. We just signed a _____ with an important customer.
2. These are just some _____ for now.
3. Could you _____ the contract and send it back by Friday?
4. You _____ them to ask for more information.
5. This document _____ right. Are you sure this is the right one?
6. The new administrative assistant is starting with us _____.
7. This _____ we owe them $300, but I think it's wrong.
8. I've already completed the _____ tasks on the list.
9. Meeting Room 4 is always the _____ room.
10. Please _____ that book – I want to use it in a minute.

> **Points to Dictate**
>
> 前 Unit 同様、音が脱落するケースに挑戦しましょう。
> 1 はビッ[ ]ディール、以下、ラ[ ]フィギュアス、プリー[ ]サイン、クッ[ ]コール、ダズン[ ]ルック、ネックス[ ]ウィーク、インヴォイ[ ]セズ、ファー[ ]スリー、モウス[ ]ポピュラー、ドン[ ]テイク、のようになります。

 ☑ 頻出単語チェック！ **Listening Section**

語句と意味を品詞に気をつけながら結びつけてみましょう。

1. approve   **a.** to officially accept something
2. invoice [n.]   **b.** a price for a task provided in advance
3. brochure   **c.** a booklet showing a company's products or services
4. quotation   **d.** a goal or aim
5. without a doubt   **e.** very big or very important
6. objective [n.]   **f.** making something smaller
7. utmost [n.]   **g.** to make certain that something will happen
8. significant   **h.** a document used to ask for payment
9. reduction   **i.** the most that can be done (*used for emphasis*)
10. ensure   **j.** it is definitely true that (*used for emphasis*)

Listening Section

| PART 1 | 写真描写問題 | 1-27, 28 |

Check Point!　2人のそれぞれの動作に注目しましょう。
主語が A woman と A man です。

それぞれの写真について、4つの説明文の中から最も適切なものを1つずつ選びましょう。

1.

Ⓐ Ⓑ Ⓒ Ⓓ

2.

Ⓐ Ⓑ Ⓒ Ⓓ

| PART 2 | 応答問題 | 1-29-33 |

Check Point!　質問文に使われた単語と同じ単語を含む選択肢に注意しましょう。
Could you sign ～ ？ → I can make a sign ～ ．

それぞれの設問の応答として最も適切なものを1つずつ選びましょう。

3. Mark your answer on your answer sheet.　　Ⓐ Ⓑ Ⓒ

4. Mark your answer on your answer sheet.　　Ⓐ Ⓑ Ⓒ

5. Mark your answer on your answer sheet.　　Ⓐ Ⓑ Ⓒ

6. Mark your answer on your answer sheet.　　Ⓐ Ⓑ Ⓒ

7. Mark your answer on your answer sheet.　　Ⓐ Ⓑ Ⓒ

> **Check Point!** 全体を問う質問の定型を頭に入れておきましょう。
> What most likely is the woman's job?

会話についての設問に対し、最も適切なものを1つずつ選びましょう。

8. What most likely is the woman's job?
   (A) Administrative assistant
   (B) Receptionist
   (C) Sales representative
   (D) IT technician

9. What problem does the man mention?
   (A) There is a mistake in the brochure.
   (B) The price seems too high.
   (C) The invoice hasn't been paid.
   (D) The invoice is missing.

10. What will the man do next?
    (A) Call the printing company
    (B) Check the brochure
    (C) Look for an old e-mail
    (D) Pay the invoice

> **Check Point!** 話し手は誰で、何を強調しているかを聞き取りましょう。
> What is special about the product?

説明文についての設問に対し、最も適切なものを1つずつ選びましょう。

11. Who most likely is the woman?
    (A) A politician
    (B) A customer
    (C) A sales person
    (D) A delivery person

12. What is special about the product?
    (A) It uses recycled packaging.
    (B) It uses new technology.
    (C) It is very user-friendly.
    (D) It is very big.

13. What will happen next?
    (A) The audience will see the new smartphones.
    (B) The company will start a recycling program.
    (C) The speaker will talk about packaging.
    (D) The packaging will be recycled.

Grammar Review 接続詞

■接続詞には**等位接続詞**と**従属（従位）接続詞**があることを思い出しましょう。

① and や but に代表される**等位接続詞**は、接続詞をはさんで左右対称となるもの同士（語、句、節）を「語 and 語」のように結び付けます。The company is expected to *increase the size* **and** *lower the cost* of the monitors.（その会社にはモニターのサイズアップとコストダウンが期待されている）。and をはさんで increase the size と lower the cost という 2 つの動詞句を等しく結び付けています。

②**従属接続詞**は結び付けるというより、接続詞に導かれる節を名詞化または副詞化し、その節自体をその文を構成する 1 つの要素に変える働きをします。We cannot promise that delivery date **because** *it is too tight*.（短かすぎてその納期ではお約束できません）。because に導かれる節 because it is too tight は副詞節となり、We cannot promise that delivery date. という文の原因・理由を説明しています。一方、I think **that** the client won't come today.（今日顧客は来ないと思います）では接続詞 that 以下が名詞節としてそっくり think の目的語になっています。

《例題》各空所に入れるべき最も適切な語句を選んで、その記号を書きなさい。

1. They signed the contract in the afternoon ------- they decided to go out for dinner to celebrate.

    (A) and   (B) but   (C) for   (D) or

2. Employees must renew their annual parking passes online ------- they expire.

    (A) whether   (B) so   (C) before   (D) due to

 ✔ 頻出単語チェック！ **Reading Section**

語句と意味を品詞に気をつけながら結びつけてみましょう。

1. specification
2. innovative
3. efficiency
4. incorporate
5. upgrade [v.]
6. option [n.]
7. specialize in
8. marketing
9. flier
10. accounting

a. the job of recording how money is used and received by a company
b. using new ideas
c. to improve or replace something
d. to be very skilled at or have knowledge about
e. a piece of paper that has information about a product or event
f. doing something with little or no waste
g. a choice
h. a detailed description
i. the job of promoting a product or service
j. to include in something else

Reading Section

Check Point! 　文法問題：接続詞、語彙問題：名詞
接続詞以外の品詞が含まれるものに特に注意しましょう。

それぞれの空所に入れるのに最も適切なものを1つずつ選びましょう。

14. ------- the weather is very hot, the manager expects everyone to wear a suit and tie.
(A) Although
(B) Because
(C) Since
(D) Despite
Ⓐ Ⓑ Ⓒ Ⓓ

15. She thought she had prepared well for the meeting ------- it did not go as planned.
(A) and
(B) but
(C) for
(D) or
Ⓐ Ⓑ Ⓒ Ⓓ

16. Joanna asked him to finish the report ------- he went home that evening.
(A) as
(B) as far as
(C) before
(D) whether
Ⓐ Ⓑ Ⓒ Ⓓ

17. After they launched some new products, he did a ------- for their biggest customers.
(A) present
(B) presenting
(C) presenter
(D) presentation
Ⓐ Ⓑ Ⓒ Ⓓ

18. The CEO told all ------- that they could work from home two days per week from now on.
(A) employs
(B) employees
(C) employers
(D) employments
Ⓐ Ⓑ Ⓒ Ⓓ

PART 6   長文穴埋め問題

> **Check Point!**   語彙問題：接続詞
> 文章挿入問題：後に続く文の意味との整合性を考えましょう。

それぞれの空所に入れるのに最も適切なものを１つずつ選びましょう。

Andreas Muller
Milan Sports Cars
239 Factory Street
Chicago, IL 23954

Dear Jenna,

It's almost the end of the year. -------. It contains information about all our cars –
19.
------- the full specifications for each vehicle.
20.

The highlight of this year's brochure is the new XR23 – our beautiful new sports
car. Using an innovative engine design with great fuel efficiency, it's great for the
city or for long distances. It also incorporates the latest computer-assisted braking
technology, making it our ------- car yet.
21.

If you would like to test drive any of our cars, please give me a call. And if -------
22.
to upgrade your car, I can talk you through the options.

Kind regards,

Andreas Muller

---

19. (A) Thank you for visiting us to test
drive the XR23 last weekend.
(B) Therefore I am writing to tell
you about our latest sports car:
the XR23.
(C) So I am delighted to be able to
send you a copy of our latest
brochure.
(D) And we're already getting
excited about next year.

20. (A) as well as
(B) besides
(C) furthermore
(D) therefore

21. (A) safe
(B) safer
(C) safety
(D) safest

22. (A) you look
(B) you're looking
(C) you will look
(D) you have looked

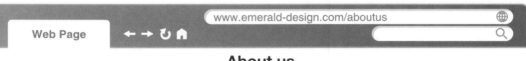

文章を読んで、それぞれの設問の答えとして最も適切なものを１つずつ選びましょう。

---

www.emerald-design.com/aboutus

Web Page   ← → ↺ ⌂

About us

Emerald Design is a highly skilled team of creative and professional designers that help our clients to look good. We specialize in marketing materials, so we can create fliers, brochures and catalogs that will really make an impact. Or we can add color and life to your Web sites, newsletters and social media profiles. See the portfolio section of this Web site to see what we can do.

Based in Richmond, Virginia, Emerald Design was founded five years ago by brothers Paul and Mark Hughes. Paul had been working at a graphic design agency for about ten years and decided it was time to start his own business. Mark had been working in accounting at a large chemical company and was looking for a new challenge.

Together they formed Emerald Design and quickly built it into one of the leading design agencies in the area.

---

23. What is the purpose of the article?
 (A) To explain a person's life story
 (B) To ask for help with some design work
 (C) To introduce a company
 (D) To advertise for staff

24. The word "portfolio" in paragraph 1, line 5, is closest in meaning to
 (A) collection of work
 (B) document folder
 (C) financial investments
 (D) similar products

25. What is indicated about Mark Hughes?
 (A) He is a talented designer.
 (B) He manages the finances.
 (C) He is not related to Paul.
 (D) He used to work for another design agency.

UNIT 4 Manufacturing

Warm up | Dictation Practice 1-38

それぞれの空所に入る語句を、音声を聞いて書き入れてみましょう。ただし、短縮形が含まれる場合は短縮形で記入しましょう。

1. Do you know _____ working on Friday morning?
2. The plant manager said that _____ meet you at 11:00 A.M.
3. I think _____ already seen this, but here's another copy.
4. I'm sorry but we _____ finished this yet.
5. We _____ usually work overtime, but we need to today.
6. If there is a problem, _____ call you right away.
7. Don't worry. We _____ miss the deadline.
8. You _____ use a machine if you haven't had training.
9. That's our factory manager, John. _____ worked here for twenty years.
10. What's happening? We _____ finished this job three hours ago.

🔍 Points to Dictate

本 Unit では Let us が Let's のように短縮表記され、発音も短くされるケースを見ていきます。1 はフーズ、以下、ヒード、ユーヴ、ハヴン[ ]、ドン[ ]は don't の t が発音されない代わりにポーズ[ ]が入ります。
アイル、ウォン[ ]、シュルン[ ]、ヒス、シュルヴのようになります。

✅ 頻出単語チェック！ Listening Section

語句と意味を品詞に気をつけながら結びつけてみましょう。

1. unload
2. manufacturer
3. machinery
4. expedite
5. be at a standstill
6. warehouse [n.]
7. move into
8. merchandise [n.]
9. inventory [n.]
10. place an order

a. a company that makes things
b. a record of the items owned by a company
c. to notify a company of the products one wishes to purchase
d. not moving or active
e. machines
f. to take something out of a truck or other vehicle
g. to make something happen more quickly
h. a place where things are stored
i. the products a company sells
j. to start living in a place

PART 1　写真描写問題

 1-39, 40

> **Check Point!**　複数の人物のそれぞれの動作に注目しましょう。
> 複数の中の1人を表す主語と全体を表すものが使われています。

それぞれの写真について、4つの説明文の中から最も適切なものを1つずつ選びましょう。

1.

Ⓐ Ⓑ Ⓒ Ⓓ

2.

Ⓐ Ⓑ Ⓒ Ⓓ

PART 2　応答問題

 1-41-45

> **Check Point!**　付加疑問文の答え方に注意しましょう。
> The yearly safety inspection is 〜 , <u>isn't it?</u> → <u>They're coming 〜</u> .

それぞれの設問の応答として最も適切なものを1つずつ選びましょう。

3. Mark your answer on your answer sheet.　Ⓐ Ⓑ Ⓒ

4. Mark your answer on your answer sheet.　Ⓐ Ⓑ Ⓒ

5. Mark your answer on your answer sheet.　Ⓐ Ⓑ Ⓒ

6. Mark your answer on your answer sheet.　Ⓐ Ⓑ Ⓒ

7. Mark your answer on your answer sheet.　Ⓐ Ⓑ Ⓒ

PART 3 会話問題 1-46, 47

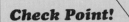

> ***Check Point!*** 全体を問う質問の定型を頭に入れておきましょう。
> **Where do the speakers most likely work?**

会話についての設問に対し、最も適切なものを1つずつ選びましょう。

8. Where do the speakers most likely work?
(A) At a delivery company
(B) At a construction company
(C) At a communications company
(D) At a shipping company

9. What is the problem?
(A) A delivery is late.
(B) The machinery is broken.
(C) The product is not good enough.
(D) A visitor is coming on Friday.

10. What does the man ask the woman to do?
(A) Send the glass
(B) Look at some information
(C) Order from another supplier
(D) Contact the supplier

PART 4 説明文問題 1-48, 49

> ***Check Point!*** 話し手がどのような状況で発しているメッセージか把握しましょう。
> **What is the man doing?**

説明文についての設問に対し、最も適切なものを1つずつ選びましょう。

11. What is the man doing?
(A) Placing an order
(B) Making a presentation
(C) Giving a tour
(D) Leading a meeting

12. What does the company make?
(A) Computers
(B) Inventory systems
(C) Warehouses
(D) Bottles

13. What advantage does the speaker mention about the computer system?
(A) It shows how products are made.
(B) It can be used to place orders.
(C) It tells them how many products to make.
(D) It checks the products for them.

■一対の語句で２つの語句、節を相関的に結び付けるのが**相関接続詞**です。代表的なものに Both A and B（AとB両方）、Either A or B（AかBのどちらか）、Neither A nor B（AでもBでもない）、Not only A but also B（AばかりでなくBも）などがあります。

------- the owners and employees were pleased with the company's new cafeteria.
(A) Not　　(B) Either　　(C) Almost　　(D) Both
（オーナーたちも従業員も、新しいカフェテリアに満足している）

頻出する形は、この例のように接続詞の一部が問われるものもありますが、相関接続詞が文頭にあった場合に動詞を単数で受けるか、複数で受けるかを問われることも多いのが特徴です。主語と動詞の関係をまとめて覚えておきましょう。
Both A and B →複数で受ける、Either A or B → B に合わせる、Neither A nor B → B に合わせる、Not only A but also B → B に合わせる。

《例題》次の空所に入れるべき最も適切な語句を選んで、その記号を書きなさい。

1. Either Tim ------- I need to work overtime on Saturday this week.

(A) or　　(B) nor　　(C) and　　(D) with

2. Not only the sales representatives but also the delivery drivers ------- now.

(A) is working　　(B) worked　　(C) working　　(D) are working

✔ 頻出単語チェック！ Reading Section

語句と意味を品詞に気をつけながら結びつけてみましょう。

1. restricted　　　　　**a.** a product made as a test
2. usage　　　　　　　**b.** to officially allow something
3. regulation　　　　　**c.** only open to some people
4. prohibited　　　　　**d.** work done outside of normal working hours
5. properly　　　　　　**e.** in the correct way
6. prototype [n.]　　　**f.** not allowed
7. accurately　　　　　**g.** use
8. assemble　　　　　　**h.** to put something together
9. overtime [n.]　　　**i.** an official rule
10. authorize　　　　　**j.** correctly; without mistakes

Reading Section

PART 5　短文穴埋め問題

Check Point!　文法問題：相関接続詞、語彙問題：名詞
相関接続詞を受ける動詞の単・複を問うものに注意しましょう。

それぞれの空所に入れるのに最も適切なものを１つずつ選びましょう。

14. Do you know ------- the factory manager is here yet or not?
(A) both
(B) either
(C) neither
(D) whether

Ⓐ Ⓑ Ⓒ Ⓓ

15. We need both more storage space ------- more staff to keep up with demand.
(A) and
(B) but
(C) nor
(D) or

Ⓐ Ⓑ Ⓒ Ⓓ

16. Neither you nor your client ------- to enter the restricted area in the factory.
(A) are allowed
(B) allows
(C) is allowed
(D) allowed

Ⓐ Ⓑ Ⓒ Ⓓ

17. We use a lot of dangerous ------- in the factory, so safety training is essential.
(A) machine
(B) machinery
(C) mechanical
(D) mechanic

Ⓐ Ⓑ Ⓒ Ⓓ

18. After the successful ------- of this job, we have another large order waiting.
(A) consideration
(B) complication
(C) commission
(D) completion

Ⓐ Ⓑ Ⓒ Ⓓ

Check Point!　語彙問題：副詞／接続詞
文章挿入問題：リストならその項目内の前後関係で考えましょう。

それぞれの空所に入れるのに最も適切なものを1つずつ選びましょう。

Warning!

This is a restricted area due to the usage of dangerous machinery. There are strict safety regulations for anyone entering this building:

1. Unauthorized entry is ------- prohibited.
   19.

2. Visitors must be accompanied by either the factory manager or assistant factory manager. ------- Do not enter the factory to try to find them.
   20.

3. All persons entering this building must wear a hard hat and a high-visibility jacket at all times. This equipment ------- to you by the factory manager.
   21.

4. Do not attempt to use equipment ------- you have been trained in its use.
   22.

5. Always use equipment properly and safely.

---

19. (A) hardly
(B) highly
(C) strictly
(D) very

20. (A) Ask at the main reception if you need to speak to these people.
(B) Both of them are inside the factory.
(C) Visitors must also sign in at the main reception.
(D) You can call him by pressing 0 on this phone.

21. (A) supplied
(B) supply
(C) will be supplied
(D) will supply

22. (A) as
(B) besides
(C) however
(D) unless

PART 7　読解問題

Check Point!　Ｅメール（１つの文書、３つの質問）
Ｅメールのタイトル（Subject）には必ず目を通しましょう。

文章を読んで、それぞれの設問の答えとして最も適切なものを１つずつ選びましょう。

📩 E-MAIL

To:	Fiona Norman <fionorman@kingsbil.com>
From:	Jerome Porter <jporter@hsw.com>
Date:	May 30
Subject:	Reflections from building the prototypes

Dear Fiona,

I am writing to share some reflections from building the prototype chairs for you last week. —[1]—

On the positive side, I think we have shown that we are able to build the chairs to your specifications, and I hope you are happy with the result.

However, as you know, we wanted to produce these prototypes in order to accurately plan the schedule. —[2]— Based on this trial, we believe that it will take approximately two weeks longer to complete the work than in the initial estimate. —[3]— This is because assembling the chairs as you requested is a little more complicated than we originally thought it would be.

So, I would like to give you a couple of options. First, I could revise the schedule and push the dates back by two weeks. Alternatively, I could request our team to work some overtime to keep to the original schedule. In both cases, I require you to authorize an increase to the fee. The first option works out slightly cheaper. See the attached document for the revised schedule and a full breakdown of the costs.

—[4]— I'm available all morning tomorrow. If you are available to talk then, please let me know what time would suit you best.

Thank you for your consideration,

Jerome Porter
HSW Manufacturing

23. What is the purpose of the e-mail?
(A) To ask for payment for a completed task
(B) To suggest a change to a schedule
(C) To request a price estimate
(D) To thank someone for their work

24. What is indicated about the fee?
(A) It is due tomorrow.
(B) It will be cheaper than first thought.
(C) It will definitely increase.
(D) It will only go up if Ms. Norman chooses the first option.

25. In which of the positions marked [1], [2], [3], and [4] does the following sentence best belong?

"I suggest we set up a meeting to go over these options and decide our next steps."
(A) [1]
(B) [2]
(C) [3]
(D) [4]

UNIT 5 Communication

Warm up — Dictation Practice 1-50

それぞれの空所に入る語句を、音声を聞いて書き入れてみましょう。

1. Can you _____ a team meeting for Wednesday at 10 A.M.?
2. If my phone rings, can you _____?
3. Could you _____ at this e-mail before I send it?
4. Just a minute. I need to _____ his phone number.
5. Let's meet to talk about the press release before we _____.
6. I need to send _____ before I go to lunch.
7. Did we _____ packages in the mail today?
8. I have a meeting _____ customer at 3 P.M.
9. Oh no! I can't _____ to my social media accounts!
10. Do you _____ use this tablet tomorrow?

 Points to Dictate

2語、あるいは3語が連結してひとつのかたまりのように発音されるケースです。1はセットアップではなく、セラップのように聞こえますね。以下同様にピッキラップ、テイカルッカ、ルッカップ、センディトアウ[ ]、アニーメイル、ゲレニー、ウィザニインポー[ ]ントゥ、ロギン、マインディファイとなります。

 ✅ 頻出単語チェック！ **Listening Section**

語句と意味を品詞に気をつけながら結びつけてみましょう。

1. a bite to eat
2. hang up [v.]
3. newsletter
4. fund-raising
5. draft [n.]
6. as it happens
7. fall behind
8. publication
9. submit
10. at the latest

a. not after (*to emphasize how important a deadline is*)
b. some food
c. to formally send something for review by someone senior
d. a non-final version of a written document
e. to fail to follow the schedule
f. luckily or surprisingly
g. a document sent to the members of an organization with the latest news
h. printing something and making it available to purchase
i. to end a phone conversation
j. getting others to give money for something

PART 1 写真描写問題

 1-51, 52

> **Check Point!** 複数の人物のそれぞれの動作に注目しましょう。
> 1人を表す主語と女性・男性全体を表すものが使われています。

それぞれの写真について、4つの説明文の中から最も適切なものを1つずつ選びましょう。

1.

Ⓐ Ⓑ Ⓒ Ⓓ

2.

Ⓐ Ⓑ Ⓒ Ⓓ

PART 2 応答問題

 1-53-57

> **Check Point!** 完了形の否定疑問文に注意しましょう。
> <u>Haven't</u> we received ～？

それぞれの設問の応答として最も適切なものを1つずつ選びましょう。

3. Mark your answer on your answer sheet.　　　　Ⓐ Ⓑ Ⓒ

4. Mark your answer on your answer sheet.　　　　Ⓐ Ⓑ Ⓒ

5. Mark your answer on your answer sheet.　　　　Ⓐ Ⓑ Ⓒ

6. Mark your answer on your answer sheet.　　　　Ⓐ Ⓑ Ⓒ

7. Mark your answer on your answer sheet.　　　　Ⓐ Ⓑ Ⓒ

PART 3　会話問題　 1-58, 59

> **Check Point!**　全体を問う質問の定型を頭に入れておきましょう。
> Who most likely is the man?

会話についての設問に対し、最も適切なものを 1 つずつ選びましょう。

8. Why is the woman calling?
(A) To apologize for being late
(B) To ask about a job
(C) To find the man
(D) To invite the man to lunch

9. Who most likely is the man?
(A) A worker at a cafe
(B) An important customer
(C) The woman's boss
(D) The woman's friend

10. Where will the woman go next?
(A) She will go to her office.
(B) She will go to the first floor.
(C) She will go to the twentieth floor.
(D) She will stay where she is.

PART 4　説明文問題　 1-60, 61

> **Check Point!**　話し手の背景（職業など）を理解しましょう。
> Who is Frances O'Connor?

説明文についての設問に対し、最も適切なものを 1 つずつ選びましょう。

11. Who is Frances O'Connor?
(A) An editor of a newsletter
(B) An organizer of fund-raising activities
(C) A worker at a printing company
(D) A writer for a newspaper

12. What is the speaker concerned about?
(A) Garrett didn't meet a deadline.
(B) She doesn't have any ideas.
(C) The fund-raising activities have been delayed.
(D) She is unable to help Garrett.

13. What does the speaker ask the listener to do?
(A) Call her about something
(B) Give her some ideas
(C) Help her with something
(D) Send a first draft today

■**分詞構文**は主語を共有する2つの文を1文で表現するときに、「分詞」が接続詞と動詞を兼ねた働きをする構文です。主語との関係で過去分詞か現在分詞かが決まります。

① Everyone was astonished by Amy's presentation. Everyone went silent.

最初の文の主語と be 動詞を省略し、Astonished と**過去分詞**で始めます。

Astonished by Amy's presentation, everyone went silent.（Amy のプレゼンに驚かされ、皆が沈黙した）となり、このとき主語の everyone は astonish される受動関係にあることに注目しましょう。分詞の導く節が後ろの節を修飾しています。

② *Listening* to Amy's presentation, I remembered my teacher in college.（Amy のプレゼンを聞いていて、大学時代の先生を思い出した）、この分詞が導く節では主語 I と動詞の listen が能動関係［＝ While I was listening to 〜 ,］にあるので**現在分詞**を使っています。

《例題》各空所に入れるべき最も適切な語句を選んで、その記号を書きなさい。

1. ------- the new brochure, I found a couple of spelling mistakes.

(A) Check　　(B) Checks　　(C) Checking　　(D) To check

2. Firmly ------- as the leading method of business communication, e-mail is now a large part of everyone's working day.

(A) establishing　　(B) established　　(C) to establish　　(D) to be established

---

✅ 頻出単語チェック！　Reading Section

語句と意味を品詞に気をつけながら結びつけてみましょう。

1. renew
2. expire
3. payment
4. overdue
5. extension [n.]
6. conflict [n.]
7. urgent
8. rearrange
9. proceed with
10. agenda

a. money paid to someone
b. late; not done when planned
c. a situation where there are two appointments at the same time
d. to no longer be active or in use
e. making something longer or bigger
f. a list of topics for discussion at a meeting
g. to choose a new day and/or time for a meeting
h. to continue with the plan
i. very important and must be done now
j. to increase the life of something

Reading Section

PART 5　短文穴埋め問題

Check Point!　文法問題：分詞構文、語彙問題：動詞
主語と分詞が能動なら現在分詞、受動なら過去分詞を選びましょう。

それぞれの空所に入れるのに最も適切なものを１つずつ選びましょう。

14. ------- to the message, he realized that there had been a big misunderstanding.
(A) Listen
(B) Listened
(C) Listening
(D) To listen
Ⓐ Ⓑ Ⓒ Ⓓ

15. Janice re-read the e-mail, ------- by her boss's decision to cancel the project.
(A) shock
(B) shocked
(C) shocking
(D) to shock
Ⓐ Ⓑ Ⓒ Ⓓ

16. ------- with our progress, I thanked the team for their hard work.
(A) Please
(B) Pleased
(C) Pleasing
(D) To please
Ⓐ Ⓑ Ⓒ Ⓓ

17. I need some time to think before I ------- to this e-mail.
(A) write
(B) send
(C) answer
(D) respond
Ⓐ Ⓑ Ⓒ Ⓓ

18. Julio has been trying to reach Beth all day, but she's not ------- his calls.
(A) answering
(B) opening
(C) picking
(D) replying
Ⓐ Ⓑ Ⓒ Ⓓ

Check Point! 語彙問題：動詞／副詞
文章挿入問題：直前の文章との整合性で考えましょう。

それぞれの空所に入れるのに最も適切なものを１つずつ選びましょう。

Dear Mr. Matthews,

I am writing to ------- you to renew your subscription to *Business Trends* magazine.
19.
Your current subscription expired on June 25 so payment for next year is now
overdue.

If you wish to continue to receive *Business Trends* magazine, please complete and
return the enclosed form. -------, you can renew online at www.modernbizmags.
20.
com/renew.

An extension to your one-year subscription ------- just 80 dollars, or you can get a
21.
25 percent discount if you renew for two years.

Modern Business Magazines publishes a wide range of magazines with the latest
from the world of business. -------.
22.

Kind regards,

Sian Sumner

---

19. (A) memorize
(B) remember
(C) remind
(D) attract

20. (A) Similarly
(B) Generally
(C) Directly
(D) Alternatively

21. (A) costs
(B) costed
(C) has cost
(D) is costing

22. (A) Your business is expanding to
countries all around the world.
(B) It is a very popular, award-
winning magazine.
(C) See our full list of titles at www.
modernbizmags.com/titles.
(D) We apologize for the late delivery
of your magazine this month.

PART 7 読解問題

文章を読んで、それぞれの設問の答えとして最も適切なものを1つずつ選びましょう。

Mitsuyo Kobayashi (9:32 A.M.)
I'm afraid I have a schedule conflict for this afternoon's project meeting. Kyle needs an urgent meeting about next year's budget.

Clive Elliot (9:32 A.M.)
OK. Shall I rearrange the project meeting for later in the week?

Mitsuyo Kobayashi (9:33 A.M.)
Why don't you proceed without me? You can chair the meeting instead.

Clive Elliot (9:33 A.M.)
Sure. I can do that.

Mitsuyo Kobayashi (9:34 A.M.)
Great. Thank you. I haven't actually sent the agenda out yet. Could you take care of that, too?

Clive Elliot (9:34 A.M.)
No problem.

Mitsuyo Kobayashi (9:35 A.M.)
Thanks. The main discussion point is that we want to find an alternative printing company for the promotional materials. Jeremy was going to find some options for us.

Clive Elliot (9:36 A.M.)
OK. I'll remind him before I send out the agenda.

Mitsuyo Kobayashi (9:36 A.M.)
Thank you for taking care of this for me.

Clive Elliot (9:37 A.M.)
You're welcome.

23. What problem does Ms. Kobayashi have?
   (A) She can no longer attend a meeting.
   (B) She can't remember what to put on the agenda.
   (C) She needs some information urgently.
   (D) She thinks the project budget is too small.

24. At 9:33 A.M., what does Ms. Kobayashi most likely mean when she writes, "You can chair the meeting instead"?
   (A) Mr. Elliot can relax during the meeting.
   (B) Mr. Elliot can lead the meeting.
   (C) Mr. Elliot can postpone the meeting.
   (D) Mr. Elliot can record the meeting.

25. What will Mr. Elliot likely do next?
   (A) Find an alternative printing company
   (B) Make the meeting agenda
   (C) Rearrange the meeting
   (D) Talk to Jeremy

Health

それぞれの空所に入る語句を、音声を聞いて書き入れてみましょう。ただし、短縮形が含まれる場合は短縮形で記入しましょう。

1. Would you like to _____ for a run at lunch time?
2. If I feel stressed, I go and _____ in the gym for an hour.
3. It's important to have a _____ with your doctor once a year.
4. I want to eat healthier food, _____ hard to make time to cook every day.
5. If you want to join the gym, please _____ this application form.
6. I'm trying to _____ early and go jogging before work.
7. I've _____ really bad cold at the moment.
8. I bought a sandwich for lunch, but I was too busy so I didn't _____.
9. Before you start running, do some _____ exercises.
10. I want to lose weight. What _____ do?

🔍 **Points to Dictate**

ここでも 2 , 3 語がひとかたまりとなって発音されるケースを練習します。
1 はジョインアスではなく、ジョイナスです。以下、ワーカウ [ ]、チェッカップ、バルイツ、フィラウ [ ]、ゲラップ、ガタ、イーリッ [ ]、ウォーマップ、シュルアイのようになります。

✅ **頻出単語チェック！**   **Listening Section**

語句と意味を品詞に気をつけながら結びつけてみましょう。

1. adjustment
2. aim for
3. as for
4. fitness
5. make a choice
6. full time
7. try out [v.]
8. nutritional
9. provide
10. refer to

a. to try to do
b. to choose
c. 9 A.M. to 5 P.M., Monday to Friday
d. a change
e. talking about
f. to test something to see if one likes it
g. to give something to people so they can use it
h. to look at to get information
i. containing things that are good for one's health
j. being healthy

PART 1　写真描写問題

 1-63, 64

Check Point! 　男女それぞれの動作に注目しましょう。
男女それぞれと2人まとめた動作についての説明です。

それぞれの写真について、4つの説明文の中から最も適切なものを1つずつ選びましょう。

1. 　2.

Ⓐ Ⓑ Ⓒ Ⓓ　　　　　　　Ⓐ Ⓑ Ⓒ Ⓓ

PART 2　応答問題

 1-65-69

Check Point! 　疑問文ではない問いかけ文も想定しておきましょう。
<u>Don't forget</u> to ～.

それぞれの設問の応答として最も適切なものを1つずつ選びましょう。

3. Mark your answer on your answer sheet.　　　Ⓐ Ⓑ Ⓒ

4. Mark your answer on your answer sheet.　　　Ⓐ Ⓑ Ⓒ

5. Mark your answer on your answer sheet.　　　Ⓐ Ⓑ Ⓒ

6. Mark your answer on your answer sheet.　　　Ⓐ Ⓑ Ⓒ

7. Mark your answer on your answer sheet.　　　Ⓐ Ⓑ Ⓒ

PART 3   会話問題   1-70, 71

Check Point!   細部を問う質問にも定型があるので頭に入れておきましょう。
What does the man ask the woman to do?

会話についての設問に対し、最も適切なものを1つずつ選びましょう。

8. Who most likely is the man?
   (A) A nutrition specialist
   (B) A chef
   (C) A dentist
   (D) A shop assistant

9. What does the woman say she often eats for lunch?
   (A) Sandwiches
   (B) Pizza or burgers
   (C) Soup
   (D) Fried chicken

10. What does the man ask the woman to do?
   (A) Eat salad every day
   (B) Stop eating pizza
   (C) Cook her own food
   (D) Give up sodas

PART 4   説明文問題   1-72, 73

Check Point!   "According to the speaker, 〜 ." の形に慣れておきましょう。
According to the speaker, why is it difficult for people to stay healthy?

説明文についての設問に対し、最も適切なものを1つずつ選びましょう。

11. What is the topic of the workshop?
   (A) Cooking tips
   (B) Exercising regularly
   (C) Keeping healthy
   (D) Raising a family

12. According to the speaker, why is it difficult for people to stay healthy?
   (A) It is expensive.
   (B) It is not fun.
   (C) They are very busy.
   (D) There is no simple way.

13. What will happen next?
   (A) The speaker will talk about food.
   (B) The speaker will talk about exercise.
   (C) The participants will read a handout.
   (D) The participants will go to the gym.

■**倒置**は「主語＋動詞」が「動詞＋主語」になることで、さまざまな状況で起こります。大き
く**文法上の理由**と**強調**によるものとに分けることができます。

①**文法上の理由**：代表例は疑問文 *Are* you a dentist? や nor に導かれる節における倒置
You don't know what is happening, *nor* <u>are you</u> trying to understand it.
（あなたは何が起こっているのか分からないし、理解しようともしていない）です。これ
は文法上求められるもので、強調の意味はありません。疑問文の他、仮定を表す if 節の省略、
as や than などの接続詞による節、so/neither/nor で始まる節、There 構文、祈願文が
あります。

②**強調**：文法的には必ずしも必要はないが、倒置によって特定の部分に焦点を当てて強調を
するものです。代表的なものには、否定の意味を持つ要素、補語になる形容詞、比較を表
す形容詞句、so...that や such...that など、副詞的修飾語句、などがあります。
すべてを例示できませんが、強調のための倒置は否定の要素の前置などで起こります。
<u>Not a single word</u> <u>could I utter</u> when I saw my father at the hospital.
（否定の要素）　　　　（倒置）

（病院で父を見たとき、私は一言も発することができなかった）

《例題》次の空所に入れるべき最も適切な語句を選んで、その記号を書きなさい。

------- started taking her medicine than she started to feel better.

(A) Sooner than had she　　(B) Sooner than she had

(C) No sooner had she　　(D) No sooner she had

☑ 頻出単語チェック!　Reading Section

語句と意味を品詞に気をつけながら結びつけてみましょう。

1. guideline   a. not likely to happen
2. from scratch   b. to remove something
3. unrealistic   c. containing things that are good for one's health
4. volume   d. very careful and detailed
5. eliminate   e. advice about how something should be done
6. nutritious   f. the amount of something
7. diagnose   g. to identify a person's health problem
8. joint [n.]   h. from the very beginning
9. thorough   i. part of the body where two bones connect, such as a knee, ankle, or elbow
10. participation   j. taking part in an activity

Reading Section

PART 5　短文穴埋め問題

Check Point!　文法問題：倒置、語彙問題：名詞
強調のための倒置は否定の要素の前置などで起こります。

それぞれの空所に入れるのに最も適切なものを 1 つずつ選びましょう。

14. Not until I got back home ------- realize that I had forgotten to buy the medicine.
(A) did
(B) did I
(C) I do
(D) when I did

Ⓐ Ⓑ Ⓒ Ⓓ

15. Maria doesn't think that you are exercising enough and -------.
(A) I did also
(B) I am also
(C) neither am I
(D) neither do I

Ⓐ Ⓑ Ⓒ Ⓓ

16. Before they were canceled, I often attended the lunchtime yoga classes
as -------.
(A) did my coworkers
(B) my coworkers done
(C) had done my coworkers
(D) were doing my coworkers

Ⓐ Ⓑ Ⓒ Ⓓ

17. My doctor gave me a ------- for some new medicine.
(A) prescription
(B) perception
(C) prediction
(D) prevention

Ⓐ Ⓑ Ⓒ Ⓓ

18. I've been feeling a lot better since I started taking some vitamin -------.
(A) extras
(B) additions
(C) supplements
(D) extensions

Ⓐ Ⓑ Ⓒ Ⓓ

それぞれの空所に入れるのに最も適切なものを1つずつ選びましょう。

Tips for Healthy Eating

Follow these guidelines for a healthier life:

One of the most effective changes is reducing the quantity of food that you eat at mealtimes. -------.
19.

Of course, the type of food you ------- is important, too. Pre-packaged meals are
20.
sometimes very unhealthy, so it's much better to cook your own meals from scratch. Doing this every day may ------- unrealistic, but you can make a large
21.
volume and freeze some for another day.

Another essential change is eliminating unhealthy snacks, like cookies and cakes, from your diet. Fortunately, there are lots of nutritious alternatives, ------- dried
22.
fruit, nuts, and fresh vegetables.

---

19. (A) To do this, you need to make sure you always eat at the same time.
(B) A simple way to do this is just to start using a smaller plate.
(C) This means not eating snacks between meals.
(D) Choosing cheaper food often means choosing healthier food.

20. (A) concentrate
(B) construct
(C) consume
(D) consult

21. (A) seem
(B) seem like
(C) seem to
(D) seem as

22. (A) besides
(B) just like
(C) in fact
(D) such as

PART 7 読解問題

Check Point! フォーム（1つの文書、3つの質問）
フォームのタイトル、そして小項目に目を通しましょう。

文章を読んで、それぞれの設問の答えとして最も適切なものを1つずつ選びましょう。

Cooper's Gym
Membership Application Form

PERSONAL DETAILS

Title:	Mr / Mrs /(Ms)
Name:	Veronica Jennifer Jones
Date of birth:	23/5/95
Nationality:	Irish
Address:	Apartment 1B, Sunny Heights, 236 Juniper Street, Phoenix
Tel:	602-776-9871
E-mail:	v.jones@kestrelfinance.com
Preferred method of contact:	☑ E-mail ☐ Text message
Emergency contact:	Simon Jones Tel: 602-885-4978
Relationship:	Husband

MEDICAL DETAILS

Name of doctor:	Callum Brooks
Address of doctor:	Brooks Healthcare, 76 Melrose Street, Phoenix
Tel of doctor:	602-345-2211

Have you been diagnosed with any of the following conditions? (Check all that apply)

☐ Heart problems   ☐ High blood pressure   ☐ Back problems   ☐ Joint problems

Has your doctor recommended that you start exercising?

☐ Yes   ☑ No

Are you interested in any of the following optional services?

☐ Fitness check – this thorough test will evaluate your current level of fitness

☐ Personal trainer – our trainers can provide a fitness plan for you

☑ Fitness classes – please ask for more information (participation requires a fee)

NOTES:

Please submit this application form at the main reception. You will also need to show some ID.

23. What does the form indicate about Cooper's Gym?
    (A) They offer additional services as well as the gym.
    (B) They require all members to use a personal trainer.
    (C) They allow online applications.
    (D) They usually contact members by e-mail.

24. Who most likely is Mr. Jones?
    (A) The applicant's doctor
    (B) The applicant's spouse
    (C) A gym employee
    (D) An applicant for the gym

25. What must applicants do in order to submit an application?
    (A) Take a fitness check
    (B) E-mail the form to the gym
    (C) Get a recommendation from a doctor
    (D) Bring a passport or driver's license

Finance and Budgeting

それぞれの空所に入る語句を、音声を聞いて書き入れてみましょう。

1. David, _____ talk to you about these invoices, please?

2. Did you _____ how to reduce the budget?

3. Can you _____ how to use the new finance system?

4. They must've rejected the proposal _____ reason.

5. Let's _____ how we can cut costs and save some money.

6. Please _____ for suspicious Web sites when shopping online.

7. We borrowed 3,000 dollars from the bank _____.

8. Please make sure that you _____ the lights before you go home.

9. Have you seen my receipts? They _____ my desk a minute ago.

10. Have you completed your expenses form yet? Don't _____ any longer.

 Points to Dictate

2，3語がひとかたまりとなって発音されるケースの最終回です。1はキャンアイではなく、ケナイと聞こえますね。以下、フィギュラウ[ ]、テラス、フォラ、トーカバウ[ ]、ウォッチャウ[ ]、アフタロール、ターノフ、ワロン、プリロフのように聞こえます。発音もしてみましょう。

 ✔ **頻出単語チェック！** **Listening Section**

語句と意味を品詞に気をつけながら結びつけてみましょう。

1. inquire about

2. consulting

3. firm [n.]

4. pay off [v.]

5. finances [n.]

6. comprehensive

7. tip [n.]

8. fee [n.]

9. late payment

10. exceed

a. a company

b. including everything someone needs

c. money paid for a service

d. the money that a company or person has

e. money paid to a bank or financial company after the date it should have been paid

f. a piece of advice

g. to go beyond the limit

h. the job of giving people advice about running a business

i. to pay back the money that one owes

j. to ask for information

Listening Section

PART 1　写真描写問題

 1-75, 76

Check Point!　2人の女性または男性の動作に注目しましょう
2人のどちらか一方と、2人まとめた動作についての説明です。

それぞれの写真について、4つの説明文の中から最も適切なものを1つずつ選びましょう。

1.

Ⓐ Ⓑ Ⓒ Ⓓ

2.

Ⓐ Ⓑ Ⓒ Ⓓ

PART 2　応答問題

 1-77-81

Check Point!　Yes or No 疑問文に Yes or No で答えない選択肢に注意。
Has the project budget ～ ?

それぞれの設問の応答として最も適切なものを1つずつ選びましょう。

3. Mark your answer on your answer sheet.　　　　　Ⓐ Ⓑ Ⓒ

4. Mark your answer on your answer sheet.　　　　　Ⓐ Ⓑ Ⓒ

5. Mark your answer on your answer sheet.　　　　　Ⓐ Ⓑ Ⓒ

6. Mark your answer on your answer sheet.　　　　　Ⓐ Ⓑ Ⓒ

7. Mark your answer on your answer sheet.　　　　　Ⓐ Ⓑ Ⓒ

PART 3　会話問題 1-82, 83

> **Check Point!**　会話中の特定の発言について、その真意を問う質問は定型です。
> What does the woman/man mean when she/he says, "〜"?

会話についての設問に対し、最も適切なものを1つずつ選びましょう。

8. Where does the conversation most likely take place?
   (A) A bank
   (B) A consulting firm
   (C) A law firm
   (D) A marketing firm

9. What does the woman mean when she says, "What figure did you have in mind?"
   (A) How much money do you need?
   (B) What will that look like?
   (C) What are your plans?
   (D) Who will you work with?

10. What does the woman ask the man to do?
    (A) Explain his financial records
    (B) Make a decision
    (C) Pay off his loan
    (D) Wait for a few minutes

PART 4　説明文問題 1-84, 85

> **Check Point!**　直接的に述べられていない内容を一言で換言してみましょう。
> What can listeners do on the Web site?

説明文についての設問に対し、最も適切なものを1つずつ選びましょう。

11. Who most likely is Vanessa Lloyd?
    (A) A banker
    (B) A Web site developer
    (C) A radio presenter
    (D) A sales representative

12. What can listeners do on the Web site?
    (A) Purchase insurance
    (B) Pay their bills
    (C) Share suggestions
    (D) Manage their finances

13. According to the speaker, what should listeners do when they go shopping?
    (A) Not use their credit cards
    (B) Plan how much to spend before they go
    (C) Watch out for hidden fees
    (D) Make a note of how much they spend

■**受動態**は他動詞の目的語が主語になるものなので、自動詞では成立しません。主語と動詞の関係に注目しましょう。

My boss *permitted* **me** to invest in that small company.（上司は私にその小さな企業に投資することを許可した）という能動文の目的語を主語にして「許した」のではなく、「許された」という受動関係を作ります。→ **I** *was permitted* **by** my boss to invest in that small company.

■**助動詞＋受動態**の文では can などの助動詞や、need to、have to のような語句と組み合わせて、〈助動詞（的な語句）＋ be 動詞＋過去分詞〉の形をとります。

■**現在完了の受動態**の形〈have been ＋過去分詞〉も、頭に入れておきましょう。

《例題》各空所に入れるべき最も適切な語句を選んで、その記号を書きなさい。

1. The accounting team ------- when the new CEO took over.

    (A) reorganize   (B) reorganized   (C) was reorganized   (D) reorganizing

2. We're still a small company, so we need to ------- in if we want to grow.

    (A) invest   (B) be invested   (C) been invested   (D) invested

3. The impact of the lack of investment in the R&D section on company sales ------- by a recent investigation.

    (A) proved   (B) proving   (C) will prove   (D) has been proven

---

✔ 頻出単語チェック！ Reading Section

語句と意味を品詞に気をつけながら結びつけてみましょう。

1. expenses

2. as follows

3. transaction

4. photocopy [v.]

5. for your reference

6. reimburse

7. revenue

8. deficit

9. executive [n.]

10. summary [n.]

a. to make a copy of a document using a photocopier

b. for one to look at when one needs it

c. the money received by a company from sales

d. money spent by employees for work that the company pays back to them

e. the amount of money spent that is more than the money earned

f. a situation where someone buys and someone sells something

g. someone in a senior position in a company

h. like this

i. a short version of something that just gives the main point

j. to pay back an employee who spent money for work

Reading Section

> **Check Point!**　文法問題：受動態、語彙問題：動詞
> 現在完了の受動態もあるので頭に入れておきましょう。

それぞれの空所に入れるのに最も適切なものを1つずつ選びましょう。

14. Some new accounting software ------- on our computers by the IT team.
(A) is installing
(B) has been installed
(C) installs
(D) installed

Ⓐ Ⓑ Ⓒ Ⓓ

15. An investigation into overspending ------- by the accounting team at the moment.
(A) is conducted
(B) is being conducted
(C) has been conducted
(D) conducted

Ⓐ Ⓑ Ⓒ Ⓓ

16. Several mistakes ------- in the financial report for the last quarter of last year.
(A) are found
(B) has been found
(C) are being found
(D) were found

Ⓐ Ⓑ Ⓒ Ⓓ

17. We're changing banks because our current bank ------- too much to send money overseas.
(A) charges
(B) costs
(C) spends
(D) takes

Ⓐ Ⓑ Ⓒ Ⓓ

18. After she joined the company, Yukiko was ------- to the finance department.
(A) assigned
(B) refined
(C) resigned
(D) signed

Ⓐ Ⓑ Ⓒ Ⓓ

それぞれの空所に入れるのに最も適切なものを１つずつ選びましょう。

New Policy Regarding Expenses for Business Trips

The new policy is as follows:

1. Transactions should ------- using the company credit card whenever possible. If
   19.
   credit cards are not accepted, use cash. In both cases, make sure you get a receipt.

2. When you return to the office, ------- the expenses form and photocopy all of your
   20.
   receipts. Submit the form and the original receipts to the accounting department.
   Keep the photocopies of the receipts for your reference ------- there are any
   21.
   questions.

3. After the accounting team has processed your expenses form, you will be reimbursed
   for any cash transactions you made on your trip. -------.
   22.

---

19. (A) be completed
 (B) complete
 (C) completed
 (D) completing

20. (A) make up
 (B) fill out
 (C) take down
 (D) write up

21. (A) in case
 (B) in detail
 (C) in fact
 (D) in order

22. (A) You must make all payments by
  the end of the month.
 (B) Please return any leftover money
  to the accounting team.
 (C) Some cash will be given to you by
  your manager before you depart.
 (D) This money will be added to your
  next monthly paycheck.

Check Point!　プレスリリース（1つの文書、3つの質問）
リリースのタイトルと出だしの1行目を素早く読み取りましょう。

文章を読んで、それぞれの設問の答えとして最も適切なものを1つずつ選びましょう。

FOR IMMEDIATE RELEASE

Contact: Simone Weiss
s.weiss@rolovo.com

Rolovo Release Financial Results

(Denver, Colorado – April, 28) – Rolovo today announced its results for the financial year ending March 25 of this year. –[1]–

Overall, the results showed that net revenue was $23.2 billion, which was 10% higher than last year. –[2]– Most of this money came from a sharp rise in sales of glass screens to the electronics industry, but there were also increases in sales of windows to the car industry.

Due to these additional sales, Rolovo reported a profit of $6.8 billion. This is a big difference from last year, when the company announced a deficit of $8.2 billion, after building three new factories. –[3]–

Chief Executive Officer Holly Martin said she was very pleased with the results. "It's been a fantastic year for Rolovo. –[4]– Our success is due to hard work by the whole team and I would like to thank everyone for their efforts."

A full summary of Rolovo's financial results is available from www.rolovo.com/results.

---

23. What type of business is Rolovo?
(A) An accounting firm
(B) An electronics company
(C) A recruitment company
(D) A glass manufacturer

24. What is indicated about the company's profits?

    (A) They are similar to last year.

    (B) They are lower than last year.

    (C) They are higher than last year.

    (D) They have not yet calculated the profits.

25. In which of the positions marked [1], [2], [3], and [4] does the following sentence best belong?

"However, this investment allowed the company to increase its production and make more sales as a result."

    (A) [1]

    (B) [2]

    (C) [3]

    (D) [4]

UNIT 8 Entertainment

⁘ Warm up　　Dictation Practice　 2-01

それぞれの空所に入る語句を、音声を聞いて書き入れてみましょう。

1. Is that a brand-new _____?
2. Don't be late. The movie starts at seven _____.
3. It was a really _____ book. You should read it.
4. How _____ watching a baseball game together this weekend?
5. Thanks for inviting me. _____ it.
6. We walked all the way to the top of the _____.
7. That was an absolutely _____ concert. I really enjoyed it.
8. If all the tickets are sold out, I _____ we could go next week instead.
9. The concert wasn't _____ the same as last year, but it was similar.
10. If you want to go, I _____ buying tickets in advance.

> 🔍 **Points to Dictate**
>
> 1語の中で音が消えるケースです。母音も子音も消えることがあります。
> 1はカメラではなくキャムラとなります。以下、トウェニィ、イナレスティ
> ン[ ]、バウ[ ]、[ ]プリシエイト、マウン[ ]ン、ワンナフル、スポウズ、
> イグザク[ ]リ、サジェス[ ]となります。

✅ 頻出単語チェック！　Listening Section

語句と意味を品詞に気をつけながら結びつけてみましょう。

1. gear [n.]
2. subscription
3. format [n.]
4. upcoming
5. superstar
6. gallery
7. outstanding
8. talented
9. substantial
10. free of charge

a. a very famous person
b. the way something is designed or made
c. happening soon
d. no payment needed
e. clothes or equipment used for an activity such as a sport
f. an agreement to make regular payments so that one can use a product or service
g. highly skilled
h. a place where people look at paintings and art
i. very good
j. large

Listening Section

PART 1　写真描写問題

 2-02, 03

> ***Check Point!*** 複数の人物の動作に注目しましょう。
> 複数の男性と1人の女性（またはその逆）の人物の説明です。

それぞれの写真について、4つの説明文の中から最も適切なものを1つずつ選びましょう。

1.

Ⓐ Ⓑ Ⓒ Ⓓ

2.

Ⓐ Ⓑ Ⓒ Ⓓ

PART 2　応答問題

 2-04-08

> ***Check Point!*** 一見すると正しそうな選択肢に注意しましょう。
> Do you ever ～ ? → Yes, I ～ .

それぞれの設問の応答として最も適切なものを1つずつ選びましょう。

3. Mark your answer on your answer sheet.　　Ⓐ Ⓑ Ⓒ

4. Mark your answer on your answer sheet.　　Ⓐ Ⓑ Ⓒ

5. Mark your answer on your answer sheet.　　Ⓐ Ⓑ Ⓒ

6. Mark your answer on your answer sheet.　　Ⓐ Ⓑ Ⓒ

7. Mark your answer on your answer sheet.　　Ⓐ Ⓑ Ⓒ

PART 3　会話問題　 2-09, 10

Check Point!　Graphic 問題では何の表かを瞬時に見極めましょう。
Look at the graphic. Which subscription 〜 ?

会話についての設問に対し、最も適切なものを 1 つずつ選びましょう。

8. Where most likely are the speakers?
(A) In a bookstore
(B) In the break room
(C) At an outdoor sports store
(D) At home

9. What will the woman probably do at lunchtimes soon?
(A) Check her e-mail
(B) Read a magazine
(C) Read a book
(D) Watch the news

10. Look at the graphic. Which subscription does the man have?
(A) HN-P
(B) HN-D
(C) BN-P
(D) BN-D

Subscription Code	Magazine title	Format
HN-P	Hiking News	printed
HN-D	Hiking News	digital
BN-P	Biking News	printed
BN-D	Biking News	digital

PART 4　説明文問題　 2-11, 12

Check Point!　According to the speaker は、その後続く部分に注意しましょう。
According to the speaker, " 〜 "?

説明文についての設問に対し、最も適切なものを 1 つずつ選びましょう。

11. According to the speaker, what is special about the exhibition?
(A) The paintings are by promising new artists.
(B) The paintings are by some very famous artists.
(C) The paintings are of the night sky.
(D) The paintings are of famous people.

12. Who is Valerie Turner?
(A) A painter
(B) A collector of paintings
(C) An art expert
(D) A movie star

13. What are listeners encouraged to do?
(A) Listen to a talk on Saturday
(B) Purchase tickets quickly
(C) Read information on a Web site
(D) Submit work for the exhibition

Grammar Review 比 較

■ **as ~ as... を使った比較**では（…と同じくらい~だ）となります。最初の as［副詞］が（同じくらい）という意味で後ろの as［接続詞］が（…と）という意味を表しています。

■ **比較級の文**では長い単語の場合は形容詞や副詞の前に more を付け **more** efficiently（より効果的）とします。**最上級の文**では more の代わりに most を付け **most** interesting（最も面白い）などとします。

■ **比較を強調**する表現にも注意が必要です。比較級に付けて **much / far / a lot / significantly / considerably** better などとします。最上級であれば **much / by far** the best singer や the **very** best singer の他に the best singer in Korea **yet / ever** などを覚えておきましょう。

《例題》各空所に入れるべき最も適切な語句を選んで、その記号を書きなさい。

1. Admission fees to amusement parks are almost twice as ------- as they used to be.

   (A) expensive   (B) expensively   (C) expense   (D) expensiveness

2. These days, games companies are expected to publish new titles ------- than before.

   (A) quick   (B) quickly   (C) more quickly   (D) most quickly

3. I've seen some fantastic magicians this year, but Ken Lane is the best -------.

   (A) much   (B) most   (C) a lot   (D) yet

✓ 頻出単語チェック！ Reading Section

語句と意味を品詞に気をつけながら結びつけてみましょう。

1. controversial   **a.** approval and praise
2. accomplished   **b.** a place where an event happens
3. reputation   **c.** what many people think about someone or their behavior
4. acclaim [n.]
5. venue   **d.** to be very busy
6. step down [v.]   **e.** very skilled
7. appreciation   **f.** to leave one's job
8. leadership   **g.** to visit
9. be tied up with   **h.** causing a lot of disagreement
10. stop by   **i.** managing or leading
                          j. thanks for something someone did

Reading Section

PART 5   短文穴埋め問題

Check Point!   文法問題：比較、語彙問題：動詞
「比較級＋than」以外の比較級の形を覚えましょう。

それぞれの空所に入れるのに最も適切なものを１つずつ選びましょう。

14. Due to the good reviews, the show is twice as busy ------- it was last week.
    (A) as
    (B) for
    (C) of
    (D) than
    ⒜ ⒝ ⒞ ⒟

15. The last article was full of errors, so please check this one ------- carefully.
    (A) far
    (B) more
    (C) most
    (D) much
    ⒜ ⒝ ⒞ ⒟

16. Marianne Noble's latest album is her best one ------- and will probably win some awards.
    (A) very
    (B) rather
    (C) much
    (D) so far
    ⒜ ⒝ ⒞ ⒟

17. The performers arrived early because they had a lot of things to -------.
    (A) appear
    (B) compare
    (C) prepare
    (D) assure
    ⒜ ⒝ ⒞ ⒟

18. The orchestra has been booked to ------- at the City Concert Hall on July 12.
    (A) conduct
    (B) display
    (C) operate
    (D) perform
    ⒜ ⒝ ⒞ ⒟

それぞれの空所に入れるのに最も適切なものを１つずつ選びましょう。

What's on: Mattheus Schwarz

This weekend, there is a rare opportunity to see controversial violinist Mattheus Schwarz in concert. He ------- pieces by Beethoven at the City Theater on Saturday and Sunday evening.
19.

------- being a highly accomplished musician, Schwarz has a reputation for being
20.
difficult to work with. Most -------, three years ago, he walked off stage during a
21.
performance in Paris, saying that the orchestra was "terrible".

In recent years, Schwarz has tended to perform solo shows, which have met with great critical acclaim. -------. One critic said that "Schwarz shows great passion for
22.
the music".

Tickets are available online at www.mattheus-schwarz.com or directly from the venue.

---

19. (A) will be performed
(B) will be performing
(C) will have performed
(D) will have been performing

20. (A) Despite
(B) Except
(C) Unless
(D) Without

21. (A) fame
(B) famed
(C) famous
(D) famously

22. (A) Most critics have not been kind to the show.
(B) Playing with a smaller group of people seems to suit him.
(C) Reviews have praised this latest show.
(D) They said the show was too long and too expensive.

PART 7　読解問題

Check Point!　テキストメッセージ（1つの文書、4つの質問）
登場人物の人数を確認しつつ、最初の発言に注意しましょう。

文章を読んで、それぞれの設問の答えとして最も適切なものを1つずつ選びましょう。

Tomasz Nowak　(11:14 A.M.)
Good morning, all. This is just a reminder to reply to the invitation I sent you last week.

Yulia Ivanov　(11:14 A.M.)
I just sent my reply. I'll be there.

Tomasz Nowak　(11:15 A.M.)
Great. Thank you, Yulia.

Brigit Andersson　(11:15 A.M.)
I don't think I got that e-mail. What's the occasion?

Tomasz Nowak　(11:16 A.M.)
It's a buffet lunch for Yvette Brown. She's stepping down at the end of the year. The CEO wants to show his appreciation for her leadership.

Brigit Andersson　(11:16 A.M.)
When is it?

Yulia Ivanov　(11:17 A.M.)
Friday at 12 o'clock.

Brigit Andersson　(11:19 A.M.)
This Friday? I want to go, but I'm pretty tied up with a few things at the moment. Do I have to go?

Tomasz Nowak　(11:19 A.M.)
No, but please try to stop by for a few minutes to wish Yvette well.

Brigit Andersson　(11:20 A.M.)
I'll be sure to do that. Thanks.

23. What is the purpose of Tomasz's message?
   (A) To ask his team to reply to his e-mail
   (B) To invite his team to attend an event
   (C) To inform his team of some staff news
   (D) To remind his team about a meeting

24. What most likely is true about Ms. Ivanov?
   (A) She plans to attend the event.
   (B) She is too busy to attend the event.
   (C) She was not invited to the event.
   (D) She doesn't know when the event is.

25. What is indicated about Ms. Brown?
   (A) She is being promoted to a new role.
   (B) She's leaving the company.
   (C) She's becoming the new CEO.
   (D) She's hosting a special lunch.

26. At 11:20 A.M., what does Ms. Andersson mean when she writes, "I'll be sure to do that"?
   (A) She is not certain that she can go.
   (B) She thinks that she can probably attend.
   (C) She promises to stop by.
   (D) She will go if she has to.

Purchasing

Warm up
Dictation Practice
 2-13

それぞれの空所に入る語句を、音声を聞いて書き入れてみましょう。

1. Please order some pens _____ pencils for the office.
2. You _____ pay with cash or by credit card.
3. _____ all, let's check through the contract.
4. They have a new sales representative. Do you know _____?
5. There are a _____ packages in the mail room.
6. Let's discuss the offer _____ they just sent over.
7. It's much cheaper _____ buy them in large quantities.
8. Did _____ have time to look through the catalog yet?
9. What's _____ price for delivery to Japan?
10. We should _____ looked around for something cheaper.

Points to Dictate

ここでは音が短く弱くなるケースを見てみましょう。1 はアンドではなくンと発音されます。以下、キャンではなく、クン。ファーストヴ、イム、ロロヴ、ザッ、ル、ヤ、ザ、アヴとなります。人称代名詞や接続詞などそこにあるのが分かりきった語が短く弱く発音されます。

✔頻出単語チェック！ Listening Section

語句と意味を品詞に気をつけながら結びつけてみましょう。

1. out of stock
2. credit [n.]
3. discount [n.]
4. coupon [n.]
5. purchase [n.]
6. sign up [v.]
7. deduct
8. additional
9. saving [n.]
10. daily essentials

a. an agreed amount that can be spent in the future
b. things (especially food) that people buy and eat every day
c. extra
d. to agree to become involved with something
e. a lower price than usual
f. to take something away from the total
g. not available in the store now
h. something bought from a shop
i. money that people do not need to spend
j. a piece of paper that can be used as money

Listening Section

PART 1 写真描写問題 2-14, 15

Check Point! 男女2人の動作に注目しましょう。
男女それぞれと2人まとめた動作についての説明です。

それぞれの写真について、4つの説明文の中から最も適切なものを1つずつ選びましょう。

1.

Ⓐ Ⓑ Ⓒ Ⓓ

2.

Ⓐ Ⓑ Ⓒ Ⓓ

PART 2 応答問題 2-16-20

Check Point! 最初の疑問詞に集中しましょう。
<u>What</u> color 〜? <u>How</u> much 〜?

それぞれの設問の応答として最も適切なものを1つずつ選びましょう。

3. Mark your answer on your answer sheet. Ⓐ Ⓑ Ⓒ

4. Mark your answer on your answer sheet. Ⓐ Ⓑ Ⓒ

5. Mark your answer on your answer sheet. Ⓐ Ⓑ Ⓒ

6. Mark your answer on your answer sheet. Ⓐ Ⓑ Ⓒ

7. Mark your answer on your answer sheet. Ⓐ Ⓑ Ⓒ

PART 3　会話問題 2-21, 22

Check Point!　話者の１人が誰であるかを問い、全体の理解を確認しています。
Who is the man/woman?

会話についての設問に対し、最も適切なものを１つずつ選びましょう。

8. Who is the man?
   (A) A clothes designer
   (B) A sales assistant
   (C) A customer
   (D) The woman's husband

9. Why does the woman want to return the item?
   (A) It's damaged.
   (B) It's an unwanted present.
   (C) It's not big enough.
   (D) It's not the right color.

10. What does the man offer to do?
    (A) Give her a discount on a future purchase
    (B) Refund her purchase
    (C) Send a new item to her house
    (D) Show her some other items

PART 4　説明文問題 2-23, 24

Check Point!　聞き手がどこにいるかを問い、全体の理解を確認しています。
Where most likely are the listeners?

説明文についての設問に対し、最も適切なものを１つずつ選びましょう。

11. Where most likely are the listeners?
    (A) At a bank
    (B) At a clothing store
    (C) At a supermarket
    (D) At a travel agent

12. How can customers receive a five-dollar coupon?
    (A) Register for a newsletter
    (B) Buy some milk or bread
    (C) Go to the customer service desk
    (D) Spend thirty dollars

13. What does the speaker mean when she says "don't miss out"?
    (A) Don't forget
    (B) Don't leave the store
    (C) Don't make a mistake
    (D) Don't lose this opportunity

■ **to 不定詞**には 1. 名詞的用法、2. 形容詞的用法、3. 副詞的用法の 3 つの用法があります。ここでは最も問われやすい**形容詞的用法**を確認しましょう。

■**形容詞的用法の不定詞の 2 つの働き**：①名詞を修飾する。②補語になる。

　①**名詞を修飾する不定詞**：1 語の形容詞なら *tall* girl や *beautiful* garden のように名詞の前に置き名詞を修飾しますが、複数語句の to 不定詞は後ろに置いて前の名詞を修飾します。
　I will buy something *to drink*.（私は何か飲むものを買います）

　②**補語になる不定詞**：The winter sale is *to be held next weekend*.（ウィンターセールは来週末に行われる）は第 2 文型 SVC で be 動詞の C ＝補語になっています。
　また、I asked you *to stop buying so much frozen food*.（冷凍食品を大量に買うのはやめるよう頼んだのに）では第 5 文型 SVOC の C になっていることを確認しましょう。

《例題》各空所に入れるべき最も適切な語句を選んで、その記号を書きなさい。

　1. Keeping the shop's outside lights on is a good way ------- more customers.

　　(A) attracts　　(B) be attracting　　(C) to attract　　(D) is attracted

　2. Everyone seemed ------- in the presentation, so I hope they will place some orders.

　　(A) engage　　(B) be engaging　　(C) to be engaged　　(D) engagement

　3. My manager told me to remember ------- some brochures whenever I visit customers.

　　(A) take　　(B) to take　　(C) taking　　(D) takes

✅ 頻出単語チェック！　Reading Section

語句と意味を品詞に気をつけながら結びつけてみましょう。

　1. catalog [n.]
　2. numerous
　3. dispatch [v.]
　4. shipment
　5. bookkeeper
　6. payroll
　7. automated [adj.]
　8. inaccurate
　9. reference [n.]
　10. on hand

　a. to send something (to a customer)
　b. a person who records the money spent and received by a company
　c. not correct
　d. a lot
　e. a book or other document that contains useful information
　f. done by computers or machines without people's help
　g. a delivery of goods
　h. a list of employees and the money they are paid by the company
　i. easily accessible
　j. a kind of book that contains a list of all of a company's products

Reading Section

Check Point! 文法問題：不定詞、語彙問題：形容詞
動詞の補語になるケースに注意しましょう。

それぞれの空所に入れるのに最も適切なものを 1 つずつ選びましょう。

14. The vendor has just sent me the contract ------- and return to them.
(A) sign
(B) signing
(C) to sign
(D) signed
Ⓐ Ⓑ Ⓒ Ⓓ

15. Our annual sales conference is ------- in London next month.
(A) hold
(B) holding
(C) to hold
(D) to be held
Ⓐ Ⓑ Ⓒ Ⓓ

16. Sean encouraged the customer ------- the car for a test drive.
(A) to take
(B) taking
(C) taken
(D) take
Ⓐ Ⓑ Ⓒ Ⓓ

17. He's feeling very ------- right now because he can't find a good supplier.
(A) stress
(B) stressed
(C) stressful
(D) stressing
Ⓐ Ⓑ Ⓒ Ⓓ

18. All spending has been frozen, so if you wish to make any ------- purchases this
month, please check with your manager.
(A) additional
(B) plus
(C) farther
(D) excessive
Ⓐ Ⓑ Ⓒ Ⓓ

Check Point!　語彙問題：形容詞
文章挿入問題：DM の最後の文章を補完する文を選びましょう。

それぞれの空所に入れるのに最も適切なものを 1 つずつ選びましょう。

Troy Connors
ASD Office Supplies
27 SE Lincoln Street
Portland, OR 97215

Dear Sir or Madam,

Here are some great items you can find in our latest office supplies catalog:

• Need help with filing? We have numerous types of folders in ------- sizes. See
  page 9.
  19.

• Looking for pens? We have ------- color you could ever want! See page 6.
  20.

You can order online, or if you prefer, you can call us on 02-7744-3344. If you
order before 2 P.M., we will dispatch your supplies the same day. -------, shipment is
free for all orders over 50 dollars.
　　　　　　　　　　　　　　　　　　　　　　　　　　　　21.

Please call if you have any questions about our products. -------.
　　　　　　　　　　　　　　　　　　　　　　　　　　22.

Best regards,

Troy

---

19. (A) vary
(B) varies
(C) variable
(D) various

20. (A) all
(B) each
(C) every
(D) whole

21. (A) Actually
(B) However
(C) In addition
(D) In summary

22. (A) I would be very happy to help you.
(B) I look forward to seeing you soon.
(C) Feel free to ask if I can help you with anything.
(D) Thank you for your understanding.

> *Check Point!*　ウェブ広告（1つの文書、4つの質問）
> 広告のタイトルと最初の段落から全体を予測しましょう。

文章を読んで、それぞれの設問の答えとして最も適切なものを1つずつ選びましょう。

Introducing Money Center 2.0

Are you looking for a simple solution to your company's accounting needs? Then Money Center is just what you need. Developed by a team of experienced bookkeepers, Money Center will change the way you record and monitor sales and purchases.

Money Center allows you to do all your financial record keeping with just one piece of software – from payroll to annual reports. You can also connect Money Center to your bank account and use it to set up regular payments.

The latest version also contains some great new features:

- *Double check* is our automated checker to help spot inaccurate data. When you input data, it looks for values that are very different to the other figures and highlights these for you to check.

- *Reference guide* is our constantly updated guidance for the data that you are working with. Providing easy access to the latest government advice and your own company's rules, you will have everything you need on hand without needing to waste time looking things up on other Web sites.

Read what people are saying about Money Center 2.0:

"Money Center was really easy to learn how to use and I love having everything all in one place." (Brad Connors, Laser Tech)

"I use it every day. It's made my job ten times easier." (Laurie Mitchell, CFJ Machines)

23. What is true about the product in the advertisement?
   (A) It's primarily for use by banks.
   (B) It's a reference book for accountants.
   (C) It was created by a financial advisor.
   (D) It's a new version of some software.

24. According to the advertisement, why would customers link Money Center to their bank accounts?
   (A) To share information with the government
   (B) To send money to people
   (C) To pay fees for using it
   (D) To monitor payments

25. How does this version of Money Center differ from the previous version?
   (A) It's much easier to use.
   (B) It contains a data checking feature.
   (C) It was created by some bookkeepers.
   (D) It allows users to create annual reports.

26. Who most likely is Mr. Connors?
   (A) A software developer
   (B) A sales representative
   (C) An accountant
   (D) A banker

UNIT 10 Corporate Development

:: Warm up — Dictation Practice 2-25

それぞれの空所に入る語を、音声を聞いて書き入れてみましょう。

A: So, 1._____ you going to do today?

B: Actually, I 2._____ set up a meeting with the people from Newman Ltd. for next week.

A: Oh yeah? Does this 3._____ the deal is going to go ahead?

B: We've 4._____ discuss a few points first, but I hope so!

A: Well, I'm very 5._____ hear it. I know you've all been working hard on that one.

B: Yes, and it 6._____ a very good deal for us.

A: So, I 7._____ and the team will do something to celebrate when it's done?

B: Yeah, I 8._____ we will – but only when it's done.

A: You'll invite me too, 9._____?

B: Yes, 10._____!

Points to Dictate

音が隣の音に影響されて変化するケースを見ていきます。1 はホワットアーではなく、t が次の母音 a の影響を受け d に変化、ワダーと聞こえます。以下、ニートウ、ミーンナッ[ ]、ガットウ、グラートウ、シュッビー、ゲシュー、プロミシュー、ウォンチュー、オフコースとなります。

☑ 頻出単語チェック! Listening Section

語句と意味を品詞に気をつけながら結びつけてみましょう。

1. advertising
2. look through
3. feedback [n.]
4. conduct [v.]
5. focus group
6. distribute
7. wrap up [v.]
8. existing
9. predict
10. profitable

a. a group of people who are asked to share their opinions about a product or advertisement for market research

b. the job of persuading people to buy a company's products or services

c. to give something to several people

d. to do something

e. making money for the company

f. current; being used now

g. to guess what will happen in the future

h. to complete

i. to read something quickly

j. opinions and suggestions on a piece of work

Listening Section

PART 1 　写真描写問題

 2-26, 27

> **Check Point!**　複数の人物の動作に注目しましょう。
> 複数人のうちの特定の人物と全体の動作についての説明です。

それぞれの写真について、4つの説明文の中から最も適切なものを1つずつ選びましょう。

1.

Ⓐ Ⓑ Ⓒ Ⓓ

2.

Ⓐ Ⓑ Ⓒ Ⓓ

PART 2 　応答問題

 2-28-32

> **Check Point!**　選択式の質問に対する答えの選び方に注意しましょう。
> Do you <u>prefer</u> A <u>or</u> B? → <u>Neither</u> is 〜 . <u>Either</u> is 〜 .

それぞれの設問の応答として最も適切なものを1つずつ選びましょう。

3. Mark your answer on your answer sheet.　　　　Ⓐ Ⓑ Ⓒ

4. Mark your answer on your answer sheet.　　　　Ⓐ Ⓑ Ⓒ

5. Mark your answer on your answer sheet.　　　　Ⓐ Ⓑ Ⓒ

6. Mark your answer on your answer sheet.　　　　Ⓐ Ⓑ Ⓒ

7. Mark your answer on your answer sheet.　　　　Ⓐ Ⓑ Ⓒ

PART 3   会話問題

 2-33, 34

> **Check Point!**
>
> 話者の1人が働く場所を問い、会話全体の理解を確認しています。
> Where does the woman most likely work?

会話についての設問に対し、最も適切なものを1つずつ選びましょう。

8. Where does the woman most likely work?
   (A) In the IT department
   (B) In the marketing department
   (C) In the product development department
   (D) In the logistics department

9. What does the woman mean when she says, "I know that's your thing"?
   (A) She knows it belongs to him.
   (B) She knows it's his section of the report.
   (C) She knows he is good at it.
   (D) She knows that is his task.

10. What will the woman do tomorrow morning?
    (A) Conduct some focus groups
    (B) Send out some questionnaires
    (C) Send the document to her team
    (D) Complete the document

PART 4   説明文問題

 2-35, 36

> **Check Point!**
>
> 説明文の特定の発言について、その真意を問う質問は定型です。
> What does the speaker mean when she/he says, " ～ "?

説明文についての設問に対し、最も適切なものを1つずつ選びましょう。

11. What is the company planning to do?
    (A) Increase sales in other countries
    (B) Develop a new marketing campaign
    (C) Stop selling products overseas
    (D) Start selling a new product

12. What does the speaker mean when he says, "some of these companies have limited reach"?
    (A) Some companies are hard to contact.
    (B) Some companies are difficult to get to.
    (C) Some companies cannot sell to a lot of customers.
    (D) Some companies have not achieved their goals.

13. What will the company most likely do next?
    (A) Look for some new partners
    (B) Continue working with their current partners
    (C) Put pressure on their partners
    (D) Establish some offices abroad

Grammar Review 副詞

■**副詞**は名詞以外の動詞、形容詞、副詞、文全体を修飾します。そしてその置かれる場所はさまざまですが、いくつかのパターンを確認しておきましょう。

① 〈**動詞＋目的語**〉**を後ろから修飾**：基本形です。

They signed the contract *quickly* before he changed his mind.

（彼の気が変わらないうちに、彼らは急いで契約書にサインした）

② 〈**動詞＋目的語**〉**を前から修飾**：目的語が長いときは前から修飾します。

The mall *newly* expanded the food court and exhibition area for families.

（モールは家族連れ向けにフードコートや展示コーナーを最近増設しました）

③ 〈**助動詞＋動詞**〉**を間で修飾**：〈助動詞＋動詞〉の場合、副詞はその間に入ります。

We send our company brochure to all clients so that they can *easily* understand the company.

（当社は全てのお客様に会社を容易に理解していただくため、会社案内を送付しています）

④ **受動態を修飾**：〈be 動詞＋過去分詞〉の間に入ります。

Business trips were *carefully* planned with a view to attracting new clients.

（出張は新規顧客の獲得を念頭に慎重に計画された）

《例題》各空所に入れるべき最も適切な語句を選んで、その記号を書きなさい。

1. The legal department must (　　) go through the wording of all contracts.

(A) care　　(B) careful　　(C) caring　　(D) carefully

2. The decision to acquire the company was (　　) influenced by an article the CEO read.

(A) strong　　(B) strongly　　(C) strength　　(D) strengthen

☑ 頻出単語チェック！　Reading Section

語句と意味を品詞に気をつけながら結びつけてみましょう。

1. stockholder　　a. a person who owns part of a company
2. proposal　　b. a document included with an e-mail
3. attachment　　c. connected to
4. association　　d. being present at an event
5. relevant to　　e. being enjoyed by a lot of people
6. popularity　　f. a person who joins an event
7. attendance　　g. a suggested plan
8. participant　　h. done to advertise and sell something
9. secure [v.]　　i. to make certain
10. promotional　　j. a group of people with a shared interest

Reading Section

Check Point!   文法問題：副詞、語彙問題：前置詞
前後関係から空所に入るのが副詞であることを見極めましょう。

それぞれの空所に入れるのに最も適切なものを1つずつ選びましょう。

14. They have been ------- buying up smaller companies to acquire their technology.
    (A) increase
    (B) increasing
    (C) increased
    (D) increasingly
    Ⓐ Ⓑ Ⓒ Ⓓ

15. Before talking with a client you should ------- check your notes about your previous conversation.
    (A) drastically
    (B) quickly
    (C) slightly
    (D) fairly
    Ⓐ Ⓑ Ⓒ Ⓓ

16. The business plan was ------- approved by the board, so now we need to put it into action.
    (A) final
    (B) last
    (C) finally
    (D) lastly
    Ⓐ Ⓑ Ⓒ Ⓓ

17. The sales representatives have been asked to visit local businesses ------- the area and promote our services.
    (A) at
    (B) in
    (C) on
    (D) by
    Ⓐ Ⓑ Ⓒ Ⓓ

18. Georgina met up with some customers ------- the conference.
    (A) during
    (B) while
    (C) when
    (D) among
    Ⓐ Ⓑ Ⓒ Ⓓ

Check Point! 語彙問題：名詞／副詞
文章挿入問題：直前の文章を補完する文を選びましょう。

それぞれの空所に入れるのに最も適切なものを1つずつ選びましょう。

Dear Stockholders,

I am writing to inform you that Diamond Industries wishes to invest in NMD. Their ------- is to purchase 40% of the company's stocks.
19.

-------, the board has been considering this proposal and believes we should accept.
20.
As you know, we are currently struggling to meet increased demand for our products. -------, we believe that investment from Diamond Industries will allow us
21.
to expand our operations and grow as a company.

We are now asking all stockholders to vote on the proposal by completing and returning the attachment. -------. NMD will make a final decision on what action to
22.
take at our board meeting in December.

Sincerely yours,

Amanda Dennis
CEO NMD

---

19. (A) achievement
(B) ability
(C) intention
(D) completeness

20. (A) For example
(B) However
(C) Incidentally
(D) Therefore

21. (A) However that may be
(B) With this in mind
(C) Apart from this
(D) Believe it or not

22. (A) All proposals must arrive by November 15.
(B) Only board members can vote on this proposal.
(C) Please submit it by the end of November.
(D) If you wish to vote, please ask for a form.

Check Point!　ウェブ告知とＥメール（２つの文書、５つの質問）
告知のタイトル、Ｅメールの Subject に目を通しましょう。

文章を読んで、それぞれの設問の答えとして最も適切なものを１つずつ選びましょう。

IRAC: Call for Presentation Proposals

We are now inviting presentation proposals for this year's International Railway Association Conference, which will be held in Dusseldorf from October 15 to 19. All presentations relevant to the railway industry will be considered.

We offer four different formats for sessions: 30-minute presentations, 60-minute presentations, panel discussions, and poster sessions. If you wish to submit a proposal, please apply through our Web site. The deadline for receipt is May 30. Be warned that due to the popularity of the conference, not all proposals will be accepted. Successful applicants will be contacted by June 20 and asked to confirm their attendance by July 14.

Corporate participants are welcome to submit presentation proposals through the process outlined above, but can also pay to secure a sponsored session. Doing this will mean that your presentation is labeled as a promotional session in the conference materials. If you wish to find out more about sponsored sessions, please contact info@irac.com.

To:	Imogen Cooper<imogenc@rtm.com>
From:	Ricardo Suarez<suarezr@rtm.com>
Subject:	March 8
Date:	IRAC Conference

Hi Imogen,

Did you see that IRAC is now accepting presentation proposals for this year's conference? This is the perfect opportunity to get the word out about our new ticket machines, so I want to submit something.

My preference would be to avoid the "promotional" label as this can put some people off, and it's always better to have a longer session as this allows us to go into more depth – and we should pitch for a normal presentation rather than any of the other options.

So, can I put you in charge of submitting a couple of proposals? Before you write anything, I'd find a couple of experts who can present something for us – if we have some big names, we'll get a better audience. Try the team from Ellesmere University who wrote that study for us last year. If they're not available, send me a list of other possibilities and I'll tell you who would be suitable.

Ricardo Suárez
Marketing Director
Railway Ticket Machines Ltd.

23. When must presentation proposals be received by IRAC?
  (A) May 30
  (B) June 20
  (C) July 14
  (D) October 19

24. In the announcement, the word "outlined" in paragraph 3, line 2, is closest in meaning to
  (A) described
  (B) highlighted
  (C) detailed
  (D) omitted

25. What does Mr. Suárez imply about the conference?

(A) It's a useful way to find out about competitors' products.

(B) It's a good idea to pay for a promotional presentation.

(C) It's a great opportunity to network with academics.

(D) It's an ideal chance to promote their latest product.

26. According to Mr. Suárez, what presentation style would be best for Railway Ticket Machines Ltd.?

(A) A 30-minute presentation

(B) A 60-minute presentation

(C) A panel discussion

(D) A poster session

27. What will Ms. Cooper likely do next?

(A) Submit a presentation proposal

(B) Send Mr. Suárez a list of possible presenters

(C) Contact some professors

(D) Write a presentation

Technical Areas

:: Warm up   **Dictation Practice** 2-37

それぞれの空所に入る語句を、音声を聞いて書き入れてみましょう。ただし、短縮形が含まれる場合は短縮形で記入しましょう。

A: Good morning, Lewis. Beautiful day, ¹._____ ?

B: Yes, it is. How ²._____ weekend?

A: Great, thanks. I met up with some old friends. ³._____ do?

B: I ⁴._____ take it easy, so I just stayed home and watched TV.

A: Sounds good. Anyway, ⁵._____ tell me how the project is coming along?

B: Sure. Please ⁶._____ and I'll show you the latest version.

A: Actually, I'm afraid I have to go to a meeting in a minute. Could you just ⁷._____ progress?

B: So, ⁸._____ know, we're building the software in stages, so we're on stage 4 of 6 so far.

A: I see. Do you think it will be finished ⁹._____?

B: Yeah. We ¹⁰._____ finish the last part and then test everything, but, yes, I think we can do it.

 Points to Dictate

音が隣の音に影響されて変化するものの聞き取りに挑戦します。以下、ポイントです。1 はイズント イットではなく、イズネとなります。ワジョア、ワディデュ、ウォネッ[ ]、クジュ、スィ[ ]ダウン、サマライジョア、アジュ、ディシィヤー、ハフタとなります。

 ✓ **頻出単語チェック！** **Listening Section**

語句と意味を品詞に気をつけながら結びつけてみましょう。

1. outlet
2. unplug
3. plug in
4. call in
5. overview
6. booklet
7. in-house
8. intensive [adj.]
9. customize
10. preference

a. general information about something
b. to disconnect an appliance or device from electric power
c. a place to connect an appliance or device to electric power
d. a short, thin book containing information about something
e. to visit
f. done inside the company
g. to change something to suit someone's needs or likes
h. to connect an appliance or device to electric power
i. doing a lot of things in a short amount of time
j. something that someone likes more than other things

Listening Section

PART 1　写真描写問題

 2-38, 39

> **Check Point!**　人物以外の状況にも注意が必要です。
> 特定の人物と人物以外の両方が主語になっている説明です。

それぞれの写真について、4つの説明文の中から最も適切なものを1つずつ選びましょう。

1.

Ⓐ Ⓑ Ⓒ Ⓓ

2.

Ⓐ Ⓑ Ⓒ Ⓓ

PART 2　応答問題

 2-40-44

> **Check Point!**　最初の疑問詞と時制にも注意しましょう。
> <u>When did</u> you 〜?

それぞれの設問の応答として最も適切なものを1つずつ選びましょう。

3. Mark your answer on your answer sheet.　　　　Ⓐ Ⓑ Ⓒ

4. Mark your answer on your answer sheet.　　　　Ⓐ Ⓑ Ⓒ

5. Mark your answer on your answer sheet.　　　　Ⓐ Ⓑ Ⓒ

6. Mark your answer on your answer sheet.　　　　Ⓐ Ⓑ Ⓒ

7. Mark your answer on your answer sheet.　　　　Ⓐ Ⓑ Ⓒ

Check Point! Graphic 問題では何の図や表かを瞬時に見極めましょう。
Look at the graphic. Which area 〜 ?

会話についての設問に対し、最も適切なものを 1 つずつ選びましょう。

8. Why is the woman calling?
(A) To find out the location of a shop
(B) To give some advice
(C) To ask for some help
(D) To order a laptop

9. What does the woman suggest?
(A) Calling another store
(B) Disconnecting a cable
(C) Trying a different outlet
(D) Visiting the store

10. Look at the graphic. Which area is the repairs desk?
(A) Area A
(B) Area B
(C) Area C
(D) Area D

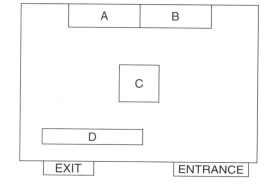

Check Point! 細部を問う質問にも定型があるので基本パターンを覚えましょう。
What is mentioned about 〜 ?

説明文についての設問に対し、最も適切なものを 1 つずつ選びましょう。

11. Who most likely are the listeners?
(A) Business skills trainers
(B) HR staff
(C) Sales representatives
(D) Software developers

12. What is mentioned about the full list of courses?
(A) It is in the brochure.
(B) It is on the Web site.
(C) It is on the slides.
(D) It is a brief overview.

13. What does the speaker mean when she says "we'll suggest a solution"?
(A) The company will answer the question.
(B) The company will recommend some courses.
(C) Her company will tell them how much time is needed.
(D) Her company will provide an idea.

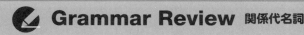

Grammar Review 関係代名詞

■**関係代名詞**には who, which, that, what の４つがあります。この中で that は which や who の代わりに使うことができる便利な関係代名詞です。しかし that しか使えない場合や that を使えない場合もありますので確認しておきましょう。

① **that しか使えない場合**：先行詞に the most, the only, all など強い限定詞がついているとき。This is *the most* beautiful picture **that** ～ . など。ただし先行詞が人の場合は who も可。また、前に疑問詞があるとき。*Who* is the man **that** is staring at me?（私をじっと見ている男性は誰ですか）は that を用いる。さらに先行詞が人と物の両者を含むとき。I saw *a man and a dog* **that** were walking ～ .

② **that が使えない場合**：that には非制限用法がありません。He had two daughters, **who** became pianists.（彼には２人の娘がいて、２人ともピアニストになった）また、先行詞に that、those が含まれるときは that を使いません。

《例題》各空所に入れるべき最も適切な語句を選んで、その記号を書きなさい。

1. This is the biggest laboratory ------- I have ever seen.

   (A) who　　(B) whom　　(C) what　　(D) that

2. All engineers ------- attend the IT seminar will get a free lunch.

   (A) who　　(B) whose　　(C) their　　(D) they

✅ 頻出単語チェック！　Reading Section

語句と意味を品詞に気をつけながら結びつけてみましょう。

1. appliance
2. malfunction [v.]
3. cartridge
4. insert [v.]
5. replacement
6. warranty
7. without mentioning
8. specify
9. back up [v.]
10. sensitive information

a. to stop working properly
b. a new thing to use instead of the old one
c. without saying anything about something
d. to put something into another thing
e. to clearly explain something
f. an electrical device used in the house, such as a washing machine
g. to make a copy of the files on one's computer in case the computer is damaged
h. an agreement that a company will replace or repair a product for free during a fixed period or time
i. information about people that they don't want others to know, because it is personal
j. a plastic container of ink used in a printer

Reading Section

PART 5 短文穴埋め問題

> **Check Point!** 文法問題：関係代名詞、語彙問題：副詞
> that しか使えない場合と that が使えない場合の見極めが大切です。

それぞれの空所に入れるのに最も適切なものを 1 つずつ選びましょう。

14. Who is the lady ------- is talking to the director of the R&D section?
(A) what
(B) that
(C) which
(D) whom

Ⓐ Ⓑ Ⓒ Ⓓ

15. Our R&D team has developed a new smartphone ------- is made from recycled parts.
(A) that
(B) what
(C) who
(D) whose

Ⓐ Ⓑ Ⓒ Ⓓ

16. Please note that all staff ------- ID card has expired must renew it within a week.
(A) whom
(B) whose
(C) which
(D) when

Ⓐ Ⓑ Ⓒ Ⓓ

17. The team meets ------- to discuss the project and help each other with any problems.
(A) luckily
(B) really
(C) frequently
(D) collaboratively

Ⓐ Ⓑ Ⓒ Ⓓ

18. The experiment failed, so Dennis needs to analyze the data ------- to find out what happened.
(A) surely
(B) absolutely
(C) carefully
(D) hardly

Ⓐ Ⓑ Ⓒ Ⓓ

PART 6　長文穴埋め問題

Check Point!　語彙問題：接続詞
文章挿入問題：前の文章と後ろの段落との整合性を考えましょう。

それぞれの空所に入れるのに最も適切なものを１つずつ選びましょう。

Dear Sir or Madam,

I am writing to ask for some technical support with an appliance I bought at your store.

I bought my printer from your store a couple of months ago. At first it worked fine, but last week, it started to malfunction. ------- I ask it to print something, the paper
19.
comes out without anything on it.

The issue started after I bought some new ink. I followed the instructions in the manual very -------. I turned off the printer, took out the empty cartridge, and
20.
inserted the new one – but now it won't print anything. -------.
21.

If not, would it be possible to bring the printer to your store this weekend for you to take a look at? ------- I only bought the printer a couple of months ago, I was
22.
hoping that you could either repair it or give me a replacement printer. The warranty has not expired yet.

Thank you for your help with this. I hope to hear from you soon.

Sincerely yours,

Roger Spears

---

19. (A) Whatever
(B) Whenever
(C) Wherever
(D) Whoever

20. (A) care
(B) careful
(C) carefully
(D) careless

21. (A) Would you like me to fix this for you?
(B) Thank you again for resolving this issue for me.
(C) So I am very happy with my purchase.
(D) Do you have any idea what may be causing this problem?

22. (A) Since
(B) Although
(C) Moreover
(D) Besides

Check Point! Eメールのやりとり（2つの文書、5つの質問）
アドレスのドメインから職場の同僚であることを確認しましょう。

文章を読んで、それぞれの設問の答えとして最も適切なものを1つずつ選びましょう。

✉ E-MAIL

To: Margaret Wu <margaret.wu@mns-edutech.com>

From: Jeannette George <jeannette.george@mns-edutech.com>

Date: May 6

Subject: Research advice

Hi Margaret,

I will be conducting some interviews with university students next month as part of my research and I want to make sure that I am following the correct procedures.

I have permission from the university to carry out the research. I will speak to each student individually and record our conversations.

I have also prepared a letter that explains my research and asks for the students' permission to video the interview and for me to use their answers in my research – without mentioning their names, of course.

Is there anything else that I need to organize ahead of my research?

Thank you for your help,

Jeannette

E-mail

To: Jeannette George <jeannette.george@mns-edutech.com>

From: Margaret Wu <margaret.wu@mns-edutech.com>

Date: May 7

Subject: Re: Research advice

Hi Jeannette,

You have done a lot of things correctly. Make sure the letter also makes it clear that participation is optional and that students can decide to withdraw from the research at any time.

It's also critical that this letter details how you will store and protect their personal data. You need to store the videos in a locked cupboard in the research office and not save them online. Normally, researchers watch the videos to write down what people said (without writing participant's names) and then erase the videos after the end of the project. If this is what you intend to do, make sure you specify this.

You also need to decide how you will back up your data. Don't just keep the files on your computer. Use a private folder on the company system – and for added security, password protect any files that contain sensitive information.

Kind regards,

Margaret

23. Why did Ms. George write the e-mail?
    (A) To ask for some advice about doing some research
    (B) To explain the results of some research
    (C) To get permission to do some research
    (D) To thank someone for taking part in some research

24. According to the first e-mail, what is the plan for the research?
    (A) Ms. George will observe some lessons.
    (B) Ms. George will hold a group interview.
    (C) Ms. George will conduct a research experiment.
    (D) Ms. George will ask students some questions.

25. According to the e-mails, what is NOT required in the letter?
(A) Information about the research
(B) Information about file storage
(C) Information about how to withdraw
(D) Information about backing up data

26. In the second e-mail, what does Ms. Wu advise Ms. George to do?
(A) Back up the video files online
(B) Destroy the videos after writing down what people said
(C) Keep the files in secure location
(D) Write participants' names on the video label

27. What is indicated about the research data?
(A) The files should only be kept on Ms. George's computer.
(B) The files should be saved on the company system.
(C) The files should not be kept on Ms. George's computer.
(D) The files should be shared with Ms. Wu.

UNIT 12 Travel

:: **Warm up**   Dictation Practice   2-49

それぞれの空所に入る語句を、音声を聞いて書き入れてみましょう。

Hi, Victor. This is Maria. I ¹._____ L.A. next week for a conference.
I've been ²._____ book some flights, but I can't find any cheap
ones and I'm ³._____ attend a meeting all afternoon. Could you
book something for me? The conference starts on the 15, so it would be best to
⁴._____ the 14, but if there are no flights ⁵._____,
the 13 is fine. Hugo said he'd ⁶._____ stay for the whole
conference, so I need to fly back on the 18 or 19. When I attended the conference
⁷._____, I stayed in the City Hotel and it was great, so please try to
book the same place. ⁸._____ need my passport details, it's in my
desk drawer. And regarding payment, you can ⁹._____ on my credit
card. If you need any other information, please ¹⁰._____. Thank you
for your help with this.

🔍 Points to Dictate

音が隣の音に影響されて変化するものを含む長めのメッセージの聞き取り
です。1はハヴトゥゴートゥーがハフトゴルとなります。以下、トライナ、
サポースタ、フライアウロン、オンナッデイ、レミ、ラスチヤー、インケ
イシュー、プリルオール、ギミアコー[ ]となります。

✅ 頻出単語チェック！ Listening Section

語句と意味を品詞に気をつけながら結びつけてみましょう。

1. make arrangements for
2. accommodation
3. aboard [prep.]
4. board [v.]
5. runway
6. takeoff [n.]
7. depart
8. make up (time)
9. anticipate
10. inform A of B

a. on a vehicle
b. a place to stay, such as a hotel
c. to get on a plane, boat or other vehicle
d. the moment the plane leaves the ground
e. to tell someone about something
f. the area of ground where planes land and take off
g. to organize
h. to think that something will happen
i. to travel quickly so that one does not arrive late even though one started the journey late
j. to leave

PART 1 写真描写問題 2-50, 51

Check Point! 人物以外の状況にも注意が必要です。
特定の人物と人物以外の両方が主語になっている説明です。

それぞれの写真について、4つの説明文の中から最も適切なものを1つずつ選びましょう。

1.

Ⓐ Ⓑ Ⓒ Ⓓ

2.

Ⓐ Ⓑ Ⓒ Ⓓ

PART 2 応答問題 2-52-56

Check Point! Wh-/How 疑問文の次に多く聞かれる Yes or No 疑問文。
<u>Are you</u> taking ～?

それぞれの設問の応答として最も適切なものを1つずつ選びましょう。

3. Mark your answer on your answer sheet.　　　　　　Ⓐ Ⓑ Ⓒ

4. Mark your answer on your answer sheet.　　　　　　Ⓐ Ⓑ Ⓒ

5. Mark your answer on your answer sheet.　　　　　　Ⓐ Ⓑ Ⓒ

6. Mark your answer on your answer sheet.　　　　　　Ⓐ Ⓑ Ⓒ

7. Mark your answer on your answer sheet.　　　　　　Ⓐ Ⓑ Ⓒ

1111111111

11111111111111111111111111111

PART 3 会話問題
 2-57, 58

Check Point! Graphic 問題では図（スケジュール）が頻繁に問われます。
Look at the graphic. Which flight 〜 ?

会話についての設問に対し、最も適切なものを1つずつ選びましょう。

8. What does the woman want the man to do?
   (A) Conduct a factory tour
   (B) Arrange a business trip
   (C) Go to Buenos Aires with her
   (D) Prepare for a meeting

Flight	Destination	Departure day
TA001	Buenos Aires	Saturday
TA002	Buenos Aires	Sunday
TA003	Buenos Aires	Monday
TA004	Buenos Aires	Wednesday

9. Look at the graphic. Which flight will they take to Buenos Aires?
   (A) TA001
   (B) TA002
   (C) TA003
   (D) TA004

10. What is scheduled to happen on Tuesday?
    (A) A seminar
    (B) A plane journey
    (C) An important meeting
    (D) A visit to a factory

PART 4 説明文問題
 2-59, 60

Check Point! Graphic は何の図（イラスト）か瞬時に理解しましょう。
Look at the graphic. Where is 〜 ?

説明文についての設問に対し、最も適切なものを1つずつ選びましょう。

11. Look at the graphic. Where is the aircraft?
    (A) New York
    (B) Chicago
    (C) Los Angeles
    (D) Portland

Today's Weather	
New York	Chicago
Los Angeles	Portland

12. What is the reason for the delay in boarding?
    (A) There were some strong winds.
    (B) The crew were not aboard.
    (C) The plane arrived late.
    (D) The runway was busy.

13. According to the speaker, what time will the flight arrive in Paris?
    (A) 11:30 A.M.
    (B) 12:15 P.M.
    (C) 5:00 P.M.
    (D) 5:30 P.M.

Grammar Review 複合関係詞

■**複合関係詞**は「関係詞 +ever」の形で表され、１．複合関係代名詞、２．複合関係副詞、３．複合関係形容詞の３種類があります。ここでは頻出の１と２を確認します。

複合関係代名詞：名詞節と副詞節になる２つの種類があります。

①**名詞節**：「～する人（物）はだれ（何）でも」の意味で主語や目的語になります。

whoever (=anyone who…), whichever (=anything which…), whatever (=anything what…)

②**副詞節**：「だれが（何が）～しても」という譲歩の意味を表します。

whoever (=no matter who…), whichever (=no matter which…), whatever (=no matter what…)

複合関係副詞：「時／場所」を示す副詞節と、譲歩を示す副詞節の２種類があります。

③**「時／場所」を示す副詞節**：「～するとき（場所）ならいつ（どこ）でも」です。

whenever (=anytime), wherever (=anywhere)

④**譲歩を示す副詞節**：「いつ（どこで／どれほど）～しても」です。

whenever (=no matter when…), wherever (=no matter where…), however (=no matter how…)

《例題》各空所に入れるべき最も適切な語を選んで、その記号を書きなさい。

1. ------- signs up for the tour will need to be prepared for some bad weather.

   (A) Whoever　　(B) Wherever　　(C) However　　(D) Whenever

2. Ben set off on his round-the-world trip, promising to call home every month ------- he was.

   (A) whoever　　(B) wherever　　(C) however　　(D) whenever

✓ 頻出単語チェック！　Reading Section

語句と意味を品詞に気をつけながら結びつけてみましょう。

1. have the privilege
2. acquaint *oneself* with
3. overlook [v.]
4. landmark
5. complimentary
6. a good deal of
7. analysis
8. cruise [n.]
9. deserve
10. itinerary

a. to learn about something or someone
b. to feel happy or fortunate to be able to do something
c. an easily recognized building or place
d. a lot of
e. a holiday on a boat that moves from place to place
f. looking carefully to understand more about something
g. a list of the steps for a trip or other event
h. to provide a view of something
i. to have earned something good
j. free

Reading Section

PART 5　短文穴埋め問題

Check Point! 文法問題：複合関係詞、語彙問題：接続詞
複合関係代名詞と複合関係副詞を見分けられるようにしましょう。

それぞれの空所に入れるのに最も適切なものを1つずつ選びましょう。

14. The hotel has a breakfast buffet, so please help yourself to ------- you want.
(A) whoever
(B) whatever
(C) wherever
(D) whenever
Ⓐ Ⓑ Ⓒ Ⓓ

15. Please give me a call ------- you are in New York and we'll go out for dinner.
(A) whoever
(B) whatever
(C) however
(D) whenever
Ⓐ Ⓑ Ⓒ Ⓓ

16. ------- busy you are, it's important to take some time off for a vacation.
(A) Whatever
(B) Whenever
(C) However
(D) Wherever
Ⓐ Ⓑ Ⓒ Ⓓ

17. ------- the hotel is quite expensive, it's in a very good location.
(A) Although
(B) Besides
(C) However
(D) Despite
Ⓐ Ⓑ Ⓒ Ⓓ

18. Take the Circle Line to Victoria ------- then transfer to the Victoria Line.
(A) after
(B) and
(C) before
(D) but
Ⓐ Ⓑ Ⓒ Ⓓ

Check Point!　語彙問題：接続詞／前置詞
文章挿入問題：直前の文章と矛盾のない文を選びましょう。

それぞれの空所に入れるのに最も適切なものを１つずつ選びましょう。

Review: The Snowfall Hotel

The Snowfall Hotel is a city center hotel in Reykjavik, Iceland. I had the privilege of staying there for a week ------- I acquainted myself with the local area.

19.

The view from my window was fantastic. It overlooked the city, with the Grotta Lighthouse, a local landmark, just ------- in the background.

20.

Each morning, there was a complimentary breakfast with a good deal of choices. I also ate at the restaurant in the hotel a couple of nights and tried some local seafood. -------.

21.

Overall, the Snowfall Hotel is a fantastic place to stay. The price was very reasonable, the views were incredible, and the food was good enough ------- make

22.
me want to dine at the hotel. Highly recommended.

---

19. (A) as
(B) during
(C) meanwhile
(D) while

20. (A) visible
(B) visual
(C) visually
(D) vision

21. (A) In fact, I ended up eating there every night.
(B) It was only about ten minutes away on foot.
(C) The dishes I had were excellent and not too expensive.
(D) The fish was also caught in the sea nearby.

22. (A) to
(B) so
(C) for
(D) that

PART 7　読解問題

Check Point!　Ｅメールと広告（２つの文書、５つの質問）
Ｅメールの最初に目的が凝縮されていることを確認しましょう。

文章を読んで、それぞれの設問の答えとして最も適切なものを１つずつ選びましょう。

✉ E-MAIL

To:	Jessica Lassiter<jlassiter@lcc.com>
From:	Miguel Ramirez<mramirez@lcc.com>
Date:	July 1
Subject:	New advertising campaign

Hi Jessica,

I'm working on a new advertising campaign that I want you to help me with.

Analysis of our market research shows that a lot of people have a negative image of cruises. For example they think that:

- You spend the whole time on a boat.
- There's not much to do on the ship.
- A lot of people feel ill on boats.
- Going on a cruise is very expensive.

I want to address these points in our new ads. I'm planning to make some short videos, but I also want to create some online articles to bring people to our Web site.

So, can you write something and send it to me by Friday next week?

Call me on 751-7765-4410 if you need any more info.

Thanks,

Miguel Ramirez
Online Marketing Director
Luxury Cruise Company

Take a Cruise!

You deserve a vacation, don't you? So why not try a luxury cruise this year? If you're thinking: "I don't want to be stuck on a ship for two weeks" or "There'll be nothing to do," you have a lot to learn about cruises!

In fact, one of the best things about cruises is that you get to visit multiple destinations. For example, our 10-day Caribbean cruise stops at Honduras, Belize, Jamaica and Mexico. Much better than staying in the same place for two weeks!

And being on a ship is far from boring. Our cruise ships have a huge range of things to do – from relaxing by the pool, playing sports, and shopping in the daytime to eating at restaurants and watching shows in the evening.

Cruises are also amazingly good value. In fact, they're often cheaper than flying somewhere and staying in a hotel for two weeks. That's because everything's included: transport, accommodation, food, and entertainment.

For itineraries and prices visit: www.luxurycruisecompany.com. We only sell direct, so you won't find us at your travel agent.

23. Why did Mr. Ramirez contact his colleague?
    (A) To instruct her to do some market research
    (B) To ask her to write something
    (C) To tell her to create some videos
    (D) To request her to call him

24. What is the purpose of Mr. Ramirez's advertising campaign?
    (A) To make people think of cruises as luxury holidays
    (B) To promote a new Caribbean cruise
    (C) To tell people about the company's new Web site
    (D) To change people's minds about cruises

25. Which of the negative views of cruises mentioned by Mr. Ramirez was NOT addressed in the advertisement?
(A) The first point
(B) The second point
(C) The third point
(D) The fourth point

26. According to the advertisement, what is true about taking a cruise?
(A) They don't usually involve visiting countries.
(B) People tend to relax in the evenings.
(C) Customers need to pay extra for their meals.
(D) They are less expensive than a typical vacation.

27. How can customers get more information about cruises?
(A) E-mail Mr. Ramirez
(B) Call 751-7765-4410
(C) Go to the company Web site
(D) Talk to a travel agent

UNIT 13 Housing/Corporate Property

Warm up — Dictation Practice 2-61

それぞれの空所に入る語句を、音声を聞いて書き入れてみましょう。

A: Do you have any other questions ¹·_____?

B: Yes, ²·_____ you provide assistance if I need to move house?

A: Yes, we do. Are you renting or do you ³·_____ home?

B: We actually own a house, but we plan ⁴·_____ buy a new one in Atlanta.

A: OK. Well, in that case, we can pay for temporary accommodation for you ⁵·_____ your old home and find a new one.

B: Fantastic. How long is ⁶·_____?

A: Usually two months. We'll also pay for two trips to Atlanta to look for housing before you ⁷·_____.

B: That's great. Do you also contribute to ⁸·_____?

A: Yes, we'll pay both the fee for moving your things and the ⁹·_____.

B: ¹⁰·_____. Thanks for answering my question.

🔍 Points to Dictate

様々な変化の混合編です。ポイントは1はアバウ[ ]ザロール、以下、ケナイアスキフ、オウンニョロォウン、セルイルアン、ホワイリューセル、ザッタヴェイラブルフォ、スター[ ]ワークウイザス、ザコスタヴムーヴィン、ザコスタヴヨートランスポテイション、ザッ[ ]ウビワンナフルとなります。

✅ 頻出単語チェック! Listening Section

語句と意味を品詞に気をつけながら結びつけてみましょう。

1. landlord
2. renovate
3. brand new
4. lease [n.]
5. residential
6. viewing [n.]
7. headquarters
8. commemorate
9. draw up
10. contractor

a. a person hired to work on a project
b. to do something special to celebrate a person or event
c. an appointment to look around an apartment or house that one may buy or rent
d. an agreement to pay money to use a building
e. the main building of a company where the senior managers work
f. places where people live
g. to repair a building and make it look better
h. to create a document or a plan
i. purchased very recently
j. a person who rents a house or apartment to people

Listening Section

PART 1　写真描写問題　 2-62, 63

> **Check Point!**　人物以外の状況を把握しましょう。人物は写っていません。
> 部屋の状態などの質問です。何が主語かに注意しましょう。

それぞれの写真について、4つの説明文の中から最も適切なものを1つずつ選びましょう。

1.

Ⓐ Ⓑ Ⓒ Ⓓ

2.

Ⓐ Ⓑ Ⓒ Ⓓ

PART 2　応答問題　 2-64-68

> **Check Point!**　平叙文＋, right? は一般疑問文と考えましょう。
> The second floor ～ , <u>right</u>?

それぞれの設問の応答として最も適切なものを1つずつ選びましょう。

3. Mark your answer on your answer sheet.　Ⓐ Ⓑ Ⓒ

4. Mark your answer on your answer sheet.　Ⓐ Ⓑ Ⓒ

5. Mark your answer on your answer sheet.　Ⓐ Ⓑ Ⓒ

6. Mark your answer on your answer sheet.　Ⓐ Ⓑ Ⓒ

7. Mark your answer on your answer sheet.　Ⓐ Ⓑ Ⓒ

> **Check Point!**　話者が次に何をするかを問う定型問題を確認しましょう。
> What will ~ most likely do?

会話についての設問に対し、最も適切なものを1つずつ選びましょう。

8. Where does the conversation most likely take place?
(A) At a real estate agency
(B) At an apartment
(C) At the station
(D) At an office building

9. What is special about the property?
(A) It has a three-year lease.
(B) It's right next to the station.
(C) It was built last year.
(D) It was renovated recently.

10. What will the couple most likely do?
(A) Buy the apartment
(B) Renovate the apartment
(C) Try to rent the apartment
(D) View some more apartments

> **Check Point!**　細部を問う質問に、特定の人物が何者かを問うものがあります。
> Who most likely is ~ ?

説明文についての設問に対し、最も適切なものを1つずつ選びましょう。

11. What is the speaker pleased about?
(A) An award that the company was given
(B) A deal that has just been signed
(C) The opening of a new store
(D) The completion of a new building

12. Who most likely is Manuel Silva?
(A) An architect
(B) An engineer
(C) A project manager
(D) A builder

13. Look at the graphic. Which building does the speaker talk about?
(A) Building 1
(B) Building 2
(C) Building 3
(D) Building 4

Building 1	Building 2	Building 3	Building 4

Grammar Review 過去完了

■**過去完了**は過去の一時点よりも前のことを表すために使われます。過去の一時点よりも前とは視点を過去の一時点に置いて考えるということです。Patricia had already left the office when I **called** her.（電話をかけたとき、Partricia はすでにオフィスを出てしまっていた）では when I **called** が基点となる過去の一時点です。その一時点までの①「**完了・結果**」、②「**経験**」、③「**継続**」を過去完了で表します。

《例題》各空所に入れるべき最も適切な語句を選んで、その記号を書きなさい。

1. The meeting about selling company property ------- when I arrived at the conference room.

   (A) begun   (B) have already begun   (C) had already begun
   (D) already begun

2. I ------- a real estate seminar until last week.

   (A) did not attend   (B) never attended   (C) have never attended
   (D) had never attended

3. Jane ------- in the company dormitory in Chicago for three years before moving to Tokyo last year.

   (A) lives   (B) has lived   (C) has been lived   (D) had lived

✓ 頻出単語チェック！ Reading Section

語句と意味を品詞に気をつけながら結びつけてみましょう。

1. within reach of
2. far away
3. commute [v.]
4. around-the-clock
5. considerable [adj.]
6. availability
7. modification
8. supplier
9. enclose
10. insufficient

a. not near to
b. a large amount of
c. to travel between home and the office
d. a company that provides goods or carries out a service for another company
e. not enough
f. making changes to something
g. 24-hour
h. to include something with a letter
i. very near to
j. the times when someone is not busy

Reading Section

PART 5　短文穴埋め問題

Check Point!　文法問題：過去完了、語彙問題：相関接続詞
過去の一時点までの「完了・結果」、「経験」、「継続」を表します。

それぞれの空所に入れるのに最も適切なものを１つずつ選びましょう。

14. When I spoke to the office management company, they said that more than half of the floors -------.
(A) reserved
(B) had reserved
(C) had been reserved
(D) have reserved
Ⓐ Ⓑ Ⓒ Ⓓ

15. The real estate agent ------- the apartment after a few months, so we lowered the price.
(A) had sold
(B) have sold
(C) hasn't sold
(D) hadn't sold
Ⓐ Ⓑ Ⓒ Ⓓ

16. She had just ------- a pay raise, so she decided to buy a house.
(A) given
(B) been given
(C) gave
(D) give
Ⓐ Ⓑ Ⓒ Ⓓ

17. Neither the real estate agent ------- the construction company is helping us to fix the problem.
(A) and
(B) or
(C) nor
(D) but
Ⓐ Ⓑ Ⓒ Ⓓ

18. ------- buying and renting a property in the city are too expensive, so we're going to commute from nearby.
(A) Both
(B) Either
(C) Neither
(D) Not only
Ⓐ Ⓑ Ⓒ Ⓓ

PART 6 長文穴埋め問題

Check Point! 語彙問題：句動詞
文章挿入問題：前の文章を受け、補完する文章を選びましょう。

それぞれの空所に入れるのに最も適切なものを1つずつ選びましょう。

New Apartments Now Available

Looking for a luxury 1 or 2 bedroom apartment?

Located within easy reach of Parkside Station, Green Hills is perfect for commuting into the city, but also ------- away to be able to relax at the weekends.
19.

Green Hills has around-the-clock security and there is a gym and roof garden for ------- to enjoy.
20.

Construction will finish in August, but you can secure an apartment now by placing a deposit. In fact, twelve of the thirty units have already been sold, and we have considerable interest in the other apartments. -------.
21.

To arrange a visit to one of our show home apartments, e-mail info@greenhills.com and tell us your availability. We'll ------- to you within 24 hours.
22.

---

19. (A) so far
(B) far enough
(C) not far enough
(D) too far

20. (A) residency
(B) residence
(C) residential
(D) residents

21. (A) So act now if you don't want to miss out!
(B) Therefore, you can move in whenever you want.
(C) Full payment is required in advance.
(D) All thirty units will be available to buy from March 1.

22. (A) return back
(B) get back
(C) go back
(D) talk back

Check Point! 見取り図とＥメールのやりとり（3つの文書、5つの質問）
何の見取り図か、さらにＥメールの Subject に目を通しましょう。

文章を読んで、それぞれの設問の答えとして最も適切なものを1つずつ選びましょう。

Office Space Available!

Contact Miranda Baxter at The Morrison Building (m.baxter@morrison.com)
for more info.

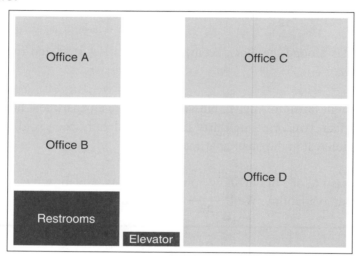

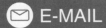 E-MAIL

To:	Miranda Baxter<m.baxter@morrison.com>
From:	Javier West<j.west@ptdesign.com>
Date:	June 7
Subject:	Inquiry about the Morrison Building

Dear Miranda,

I'm writing to ask about the office space at the Morrison Building.

We're interested in one of the smaller spaces that are available. However, I want to know if you are able to make any modifications for us. We would like to insert some walls to create three offices for senior staff. Is this possible?

Also, we need meeting rooms for regular meetings with clients, so are there any shared meeting rooms in the building? If so, how many and is there a cost to use them?

Kind regards,

Javier West
Office Manager
Purple Tiger Design

E-mail

To: Javier West<j.west@ptdesign.com>

From: Miranda Baxter<m.baxter@morrison.com>

Date: June 8

Subject: Re: Inquiry about the Morrison Building

Dear Javier,

We do permit clients to make modifications to our existing office spaces, but this work must be paid for by the client and the office must be returned to its original layout when you leave. We have a preferred supplier that will carry out the work for you. They can put up walls to divide a space into offices or other rooms for you. I have enclosed a price list for your reference.

Regarding meeting rooms, we have three, which can be booked up to a week in advance and require an additional fee. However, to be honest, they are frequently in use so I am not sure if this will suit your needs. One of our other tenants created a meeting room within their office space so that they have access whenever they need it. If this is something that you wish to do, I think the three smaller spaces are all likely insufficient for three offices and a decent size meeting room.

Please feel free to ask if you have any other questions and I'd be very happy to set up a tour of the four available spaces.

Kind regards,

Miranda Baxter

23. What is the purpose of the first e-mail?
    (A) To request some changes to an office
    (B) To confirm the suitability of a building
    (C) To promote some office space
    (D) To reserve a room for a meeting

24. In the second e-mail, what is indicated about customizing the office space?
   (A) The building owner will do it free of charge.
   (B) It is not permitted by the building owner.
   (C) The client can choose a supplier to do the work.
   (D) Purple Tiger Design will need to pay for this.

25. What is suggested about the meeting rooms in the Morrison Building?
   (A) They are often unavailable.
   (B) They are not very big.
   (C) They can be used for free.
   (D) They cannot be reserved.

26. What additional information has Ms. Baxter provided with her e-mail?
   (A) A video tour of the office space that is currently available
   (B) Contact details for a supplier who can customize the office space
   (C) Information about the cost of modifying the office space
   (D) A booking form for the shared meeting rooms

27. According to Ms. Baxter, which office should Mr. West choose?
   (A) Office A
   (B) Office B
   (C) Office C
   (D) Office D

Personnel

Warm up — Dictation Practice 2-73

それぞれの空所に入る語句を、音声を聞いて書き入れてみましょう。ただし、短縮形が含まれる場合は短縮形で記入しましょう。

Hi, Zara. This is Paula West. 1._____ attending an interview with you at 11 o'clock this morning, but unfortunately my train 2._____ by a problem with a signal, so I won't be able to 3._____. In fact, at the moment, I'm not sure when the train will start moving again, so I don't know what time 4._____ get to your office. 5._____ update you as soon as there are any announcements. However, since it seems like 6._____, would you 7._____ my interview for another day? 8._____ on Wednesday, but 9._____ Thursday or Friday, so please let me know 10._____ convenient for you. I'm very sorry about this.

🔍 Points to Dictate

アイムサポーズタビ、アズビンディレィ [ ]、メイキドンタイム、アイルビイィボル、アイルコールバッ [ ] トゥー、ゼアルビーアロングディレイ、ビエィボトゥリスケジュー [ ]、ハフトテイカナイグザム、アイムフリーオルデイオン、イフイーザラアヴズィーズデイズィズとなります。

☑ 頻出単語チェック！ Listening Section

語句と意味を品詞に気をつけながら結びつけてみましょう。

1. currently
2. expectation
3. qualification
4. facilitation
5. assign
6. mentor [n.]
7. on the job
8. applicant
9. resume [n.]
10. candidate

a. a person who may be given a job at a company
b. to give someone a particular task
c. a course that someone completed or an exam that someone passed
d. a document that lists someone's career history
e. the feeling that something will happen
f. someone who has applied for a job
g. guiding or leading
h. while working
i. at the moment; now
j. a senior person who provides career advice

Listening Section

PART 1 　写真描写問題
 2-74, 75

> **Check Point!** 　人物も写っているのに人物以外が問われます。
> 全体の状況を即座に把握し、何が主語かに注意しましょう。

それぞれの写真について、4つの説明文の中から最も適切なものを1つずつ選びましょう。

1.

Ⓐ Ⓑ Ⓒ Ⓓ

2.
Ⓐ Ⓑ Ⓒ Ⓓ

PART 2 　応答問題
 2-76-80

> **Check Point!** 　完了形の質問に対する時制の異なる回答に注意しましょう。
> <u>Have you been</u> 〜 ? → <u>We're</u> 〜 ing.

それぞれの設問の応答として最も適切なものを1つずつ選びましょう。

3. Mark your answer on your answer sheet. 　Ⓐ Ⓑ Ⓒ

4. Mark your answer on your answer sheet. 　Ⓐ Ⓑ Ⓒ

5. Mark your answer on your answer sheet. 　Ⓐ Ⓑ Ⓒ

6. Mark your answer on your answer sheet. 　Ⓐ Ⓑ Ⓒ

7. Mark your answer on your answer sheet. 　Ⓐ Ⓑ Ⓒ

> *Check Point!* 登場人物が３人の会話問題があることを覚えておきましょう。
> What are the men ～ ?

会話についての設問に対し、最も適切なものを１つずつ選びましょう。

8. Who most likely is the woman?
(A) An applicant for a job
(B) A member of the personnel department
(C) The head of the legal department
(D) A business skills trainer

9. What are the men optimistic about?
(A) The woman's success
(B) The company's success
(C) The mentor scheme's success
(D) The training course's success

10. What does the woman ask about?
(A) Mentors
(B) Availability
(C) Salary
(D) Training

PART 4 説明文問題 2-83, 84

> *Check Point!* 聞き手が次にとるであろう行動を予測する質問があります。
> What will the listeners most likely do next?

説明文についての設問に対し、最も適切なものを１つずつ選びましょう。

11. Who most likely are the listeners?
(A) Customer service staff
(B) Job applicants
(C) Members of the HR team
(D) Interview candidates

12. Look at the graphic. For which stage will the dates be changed?
(A) Stage 1
(B) Stage 2
(C) Stage 3
(D) Stage 4

13. What will the listeners most likely do next?
(A) They will write something.
(B) They will review some documents.
(C) They will attend the first round of interviews.
(D) They will attend the second round of interviews.

Stage	Dates
Stage 1: Post job ad	May 31
Stage 2: Review resumes	June 15 to 30
Stage 3: First round of interviews	July 7 to 14
Stage 4: Second round of interviews	August 4

⚡ Grammar Review 使 役

■「**使役**」の基本は SVOC の第 5 文型をとるということです。ある行為を他人にさせることから「使役」と呼ばれます。使役動詞には **make**「（強制的に）～させる」、**have**「（当然のことを）してもらう」、**let**「（自由に）～させる、～するのを許す」の 3 つがあります。他に同じような働きをする get と help を加えて 5 つと考えることもあります。

補語には原形不定詞、不定詞、現在分詞、過去分詞をとりますが、動詞によって補語となるものが変わる点に注意しましょう。例えば、make, have, let は to 不定詞を補語にとれませんが、get と help は to 不定詞をとるなどです。

《例題》各空所に入れるべき最も適切な語句を選んで、その記号を書きなさい。

1. Poor results during the winter season made the CEO ------- our sales team.

   (A) downsize　　(B) to downsize　　(C) downsized　　(D) downsizing

2. The Personnel Department has all new employees ------- for three days when they start.

   (A) training　　(B) to train　　(C) trained　　(D) train

3. Could you get Ms. Burney ------- the training report by Friday morning?

   (A) finish　　(B) finishing　　(C) to finish　　(D) finished

✓ 頻出単語チェック！　**Reading Section**

語句と意味を品詞に気をつけながら結びつけてみましょう。

1. job opening
2. public relations
3. press release
4. as requested
5. inconvenience [n.]
6. hectic
7. sick leave
8. slot [n.]
9. certificate [n.]
10. recruitment

a. following one's request
b. very busy
c. a need for someone to work at a company
d. a document given to the media by a company to announce something
e. time off work because of illness
f. the job of communicating news about the company to people outside the company
g. an amount of time for an appointment
h. finding new people to work at a company
i. causing problems for someone
j. a piece of paper that is an official record of passing a course or exam

PART 5 短文穴埋め問題

Check Point! 文法問題：使役、語彙問題：関係代名詞
make, have, let の3つの使役動詞を見逃さないようにしましょう。

それぞれの空所に入れるのに最も適切なものを1つずつ選びましょう。

14. I need you to ------- Simon to prepare the tasks for the interviews next week.
(A) have
(B) make
(C) help
(D) let

15. My manager makes me ------- him at the end of each day to tell him what I have done.
(A) e-mails
(B) e-mailing
(C) e-mailed
(D) e-mail

16. Please have everyone on your team ------- for one of the software training sessions next week.
(A) signs up
(B) sign up
(C) signing up
(D) signed up

17. We've set up interviews with three candidates, ------- all have excellent resumes.
(A) who
(B) which
(C) that
(D) where

18. The company offered him a job ------- was much better paid than his current position.
(A) when
(B) what
(C) that
(D) where

PART 6   長文穴埋め問題

> **Check Point!**　語彙問題：名詞／動詞
> 文章挿入問題：前後関係の中で整合性のある文を選びましょう。

それぞれの空所に入れるのに最も適切なものを１つずつ選びましょう。

PR Officer

A large environmental organization has an exciting job opening for a Public Relations officer. The PR team is urgently seeking an experienced ------- to write
19.
press releases and work with the media to share updates about the work of the organization.

Prior experience of working with the media is highly desirable. -------. The same
20.
applies to experience of social media marketing.

As a full-time -------, you will receive monthly pension contributions and an
21.
allowance of fifteen days of vacation per year. Salary depends on experience.

For more information, ------- Jim McDonald on 212-665-8923 or at jmcdonald@
22.
newyorkrecruitment.com.

---

19. (A) professional
(B) qualification
(C) background
(D) position

20. (A) They're looking for someone
with existing contacts.
(B) They would prefer someone who
has published articles before.
(C) You must be an experienced and
skilled writer.
(D) The ability to write well is a must.

21. (A) employ
(B) employee
(C) employer
(D) employment

22. (A) contact
(B) speak
(C) e-mail
(D) talk

Check Point! スケジュールと E メールのやりとり（3 つの文書、5 つの質問）
何のスケジュールか、さらに E メールの Subject に目を通しましょう。

文章を読んで、それぞれの設問の答えとして最も適切なものを 1 つずつ選びましょう。

✉ E-MAIL

To: Amira Khalid<akhalid@psj.com>
From: Harry Newman<hnewman@psj.com>
Date: September 3
Subject: Interview schedule

Hi Amira,

Following our discussion about your availability, I'm sending you the schedule for the second-round interviews – as well as resumes for all the candidates. Will one of the assistant directors from the project office also attend the interview? If so, please let me know who and I will send the information to them, too.

After interviewing 18 applicants in the first round, we found there were six very promising candidates, so I'm confident that you will be able to find someone.

As requested, I have sent each candidate the scheduling task and asked them to bring it to the interview for discussion. They have also been asked to bring some example documents from real projects they have managed.

Please ask if you have any questions.

Kind regards,

Harry Newman
HR Officer
Parker, Shaw & Jones

Interview Schedule

Date	Time	Candidate
Tues September 10	10:30 A.M.	Teresa Hunter
Tues September 10	2:30 P.M.	Riko Tanaka
Wed September 11	10:00 A.M.	Marcus Porter
Wed September 11	1:00 P.M.	Wesley Anderson
Fri September 13	9:00 A.M.	Gillian O'Connor
Fri September 13	11:00 A.M.	Helmut Meyer

E-mail

To: Harry Newman<hnewman@psj.com>

From: Amira Khalid<akhalid@psj.com>

Date: September 4

Subject: Re: Interview schedule

Hi Harry,

Unfortunately, I'm going to be tied up with something important all afternoon on Wednesday. Sorry for the inconvenience. It's pretty hectic at the moment – especially as our administrative assistant is on sick leave at the moment.

So, let me offer some replacement times for that slot. How about Monday afternoon, Thursday morning after 10:00 A.M., or anytime on Friday afternoon?

I also have a request: Could you ask each candidate to bring certificates for their project management qualifications? In my experience, it's better to get these at the interview stage as I've been let down before by someone who claimed to have a qualification, but actually never took the exam!

Thank you again for all your help with the recruitment for this role.

Best regards,

Amira Khalid
Project Office Director
Parker, Shaw & Jones

23. What is the purpose of the first e-mail?
   (A) To apologize to Ms. Khalid about something
   (B) To ask Ms. Khalid about something
   (C) To request Ms. Khalid to do something
   (D) To notify Ms. Khalid about something

24. What position are they recruiting for?
   (A) Administrative assistant
   (B) Project manager
   (C) Assistant director of the project office
   (D) Director of the project office

25. In the second e-mail, the phrase "let down" in paragraph 3, line 4, is closest in meaning to
   (A) deceived
   (B) disappointed
   (C) compromised
   (D) allowed

26. Which candidate's interview time did Ms. Khalid request to have changed?
   (A) Riko Tanaka's
   (B) Marcus Porter's
   (C) Wesley Anderson's
   (D) Helmut Meyer's

27. What are candidates NOT required to bring to the interview?
   (A) Their latest resume
   (B) Proof of their qualifications
   (C) Examples of their work
   (D) A schedule that they have created

TOEIC 重要熟語 100

1	☐	cope with	〜に対処する
2	☐	drop off	減る
3	☐	set out	〜を出発させる
4	☐	be qualified for	〜に適任である
5	☐	put away	〜を片づける
6	☐	count on	頼る、あてにする
7	☐	be liable for	〜の責任がある
8	☐	take advantage of	〜を利用する
9	☐	get rid of	〜を取り除く
10	☐	be through with	〜を終える
11	☐	acount for	〜を説明する
12	☐	work out	〜を解決する
13	☐	rush to	〜に殺到する
14	☐	lay off	〜を一時解雇する
15	☐	let down	〜を失望させる
16	☐	as to	〜に関して
17	☐	put aside	わきに置く
18	☐	give away	〜を与える
19	☐	make up for	〜の埋め合わせをする
20	☐	take effect	（法律などが）効力を生じる
21	☐	stay away from	〜に近づかないでいる
22	☐	take a chance	一か八かやってみる
23	☐	wear out	〜を使い古す
24	☐	hook up	接続される
25	☐	rule out	〜を除外する
26	☐	look over	〜にざっと目を通す
27	☐	on and off	断続的に
28	☐	take over	〜を買収する、〜を引き継ぐ
29	☐	go bankrupt	破産する
30	☐	take down	〜を書き取る
31	☐	give out	〜を配る
32	☐	prior to	〜に先立って
33	☐	sort out	〜を分類する
34	☐	call it a day	一日の仕事を切り上げる
35	☐	be accused of	〜で告訴されている、〜の理由で避難される
36	☐	interfere with	〜の邪魔をする
37	☐	be eligible for	〜に選ばれる資格がある
38	☐	be impatient with	（人）にいらいらする
39	☐	send off	（人）を送り出す
40	☐	enroll in	〜に入学する、入会する
41	☐	call off	〜を取り消す、中止する
42	☐	by all means	ぜひとも
43	☐	in charge of	〜を担当して
44	☐	for the benefit of	〜のために
45	☐	without notice	予告なしに
46	☐	hand in	〜を提出する
47	☐	in commemoration of	〜を記念して
48	☐	in all respects	全ての点で
49	☐	go into effect	発効する、実施される
50	☐	tear down	〜を取り壊す、打ち砕く

51	☐	approve of	~を承認する
52	☐	wipe out	~を全滅させる
53	☐	attribute *A* to *B*	A の結果を B のせいにする
54	☐	be subject to	~を条件とする
55	☐	consult with	~に相談する
56	☐	aim at	~することを目指す
57	☐	clear up	~を解決する
58	☐	in compliance with	~に従って
59	☐	familiarize *oneself* with	~に精通する
60	☐	on file	整理されて、記録されて
61	☐	proceed to	~に向かって進む
62	☐	in cooperation with	~と協力して
63	☐	lock in	（厄介な事態など）に陥れる
64	☐	in service	利用できる
65	☐	pull off	（困難なこと）をやり遂げる
66	☐	sell off	~を売り払う
67	☐	send in	（申請書など）を提出する
68	☐	stand behind	を支持する
69	☐	make a charge for	~の代金を請求する
70	☐	to the full extent	最大限に
71	☐	conflict with	と相いれない
72	☐	insist on	を主張する
73	☐	be reluctant to do	いやがって、気が進まなくて
74	☐	in terms of	~の観点から見ると
75	☐	as of	~の時点で
76	☐	for the time being	当面は
77	☐	by means of	（方法など）を用いて
78	☐	in excess of	~を超過して
79	☐	be accompanied by	~が伴う
80	☐	for reference	参考までに
81	☐	in reference to	~に関して
82	☐	go about	（仕事など）に取りかかる
83	☐	on the basis of	~に基づいて
84	☐	keep track of	に注意を払う
85	☐	in response to	~に応じて
86	☐	confer with	と協議する
87	☐	set aside	（金・時間など）を取っておく
88	☐	contrary to	に反して
89	☐	wind up	（病など）に行きつく
90	☐	in view of	~を考慮して
91	☐	at the conclusion of	（行事など）の終わりに
92	☐	settle for	を受け入れる
93	☐	in consideration of	を考慮して
94	☐	compensate *A* for *B*	A（人）に B に対する補償をする
95	☐	turn up	（紛失物が）見つかる
96	☐	inclusive of	を含めて
97	☐	live up to	（期待など）に応える
98	☐	on the go	働きづめで
99	☐	at the expense of	~を犠牲にして
100	☐	put forward	（提案など）を提出する

TEXT PRODUCTION STAFF

edited by	編集
Mitsugu Shishido	宍戸　貢
Hiromi Oota	太田　裕美

cover design by	表紙デザイン
Nobuyoshi Fujino	藤野　伸芳

text design by	本文デザイン
Nobuyoshi Fujino	藤野　伸芳

CD PRODUCTION STAFF

narrated by	吹き込み者
Dominic Allen (AmE)	ドミニク・アレン（アメリカ英語）
Ann Slater (AmE)	アン・スレーター（アメリカ英語）
Iain Gibb (CnE)	イアン・ギブ（カナダ英語）
Emma Howard (BrE)	エマ・ハワード（イギリス英語）

BEST PRACTICE FOR THE TOEIC® L&R TEST
—Advanced—

TOEIC® L&R TESTへの総合アプローチ —Advanced—

2023年1月20日　初版発行
2024年2月20日　第4刷発行

著　者　吉塚　弘
　　　　Graham Skerritt

発行者　佐野　英一郎

発行所　株式会社 成美堂
　　　　〒101-0052　東京都千代田区神田小川町3-22
　　　　TEL 03-3291-2261　FAX 03-3293-5490
　　　　https://www.seibido.co.jp

印刷・製本　倉敷印刷株式会社

ISBN 978-4-7919-7270-8　　　　　　　　　　Printed in Japan